Fierce Love

Fierce Love

A MEMOIR OF FAMILY, FAITH, AND PURPOSE

SONYA CURRY
WITH ALAN EISENSTOCK

HarperOne
An Imprint of HarperCollins*Publishers*

HarperCollins books may be purchased for educational, business, or sales promotional use. For information, please email the Special Markets Department at SPsales@harper collins.com.

FIRST EDITION

Library of Congress Cataloging-in-Publication Data has been applied for.

ISBN 978-0-06-305148-5

22 23 24 25 26   LSC   10 9 8 7 6 5 4 3 2 1

To my Abba Father,
"For from Him and through Him and to Him are all things.
To Him be glory forever. Amen."
—Romans 11:36

Every good thing that ever happens
Happens from the inside out.

—*Jessie Buckley*

Contents

Bad Mother

I SIT at our long kitchen table, my hands folded, breathing in the rare, luxurious quiet. I close my eyes and inhale the silence. I bask in it. I savor this silence. I am not used to it. We don't usually experience much quiet around here. With three kids coming and going, swooping in and out of rooms, basketballs bouncing, friends trailing, doors closing, footsteps thundering up and down stairs, laughter, shouting, singing pummeling the air, the mere *idea* of silence—the remote possibility of it—rarely nudges its way into my consciousness. At least not during the day. At night, when Dell's on the road and the children have fallen asleep, well, that's a different story. Then silence descends. I will seek it out, walk into it, and enfold myself inside it, losing myself in the quiet and the dark of the house.

This day, on this late Friday afternoon in 2009, I think about Sunday. I consider whether I can plot an escape between church services for some "me time" and sneak out to the movies. I decide

I'll make a game-time decision. I lean my elbows on the table, lower my head, close my eyes, and take in this silence, trying to hold on to the quiet for as long as I can. I try to clear my head of clutter, force my mind to go blank. I can't manage it. I'm too antsy. Thoughts of what to make for dinner seep in. I see a Caesar salad, frozen lasagna, Texas toast. I bat those thoughts away, or try to. I whisper a line of Scripture, thanking God for this moment, for this rest, for this quiet—

"Mom?"

Sydel, fourteen, my youngest, sprints into the room and lands on the chair opposite me. We Currys move quickly and with purpose. We don't usually run in the house—I'm always asking the kids to slow down—but we enter rooms at a good clip. We *arrive*, even if we have no particular purpose in mind, even if we're simply entering the room.

I slowly open my eyes and take in my daughter's face. She leans into me, her eyes ablaze. She has something she needs to say. I see her formulating her thoughts. Searching for the right words. Doing a rewrite in her mind. I can feel her anticipation. Yes, she has something on her mind. An ask.

She hesitates before she speaks. I know I am about to be hit with something that I'm not going to like. I can feel it.

Get ready, Sonya.

Sydel has been busy lately, scrambling to find her place at her new school, Charlotte Christian. She has thrown herself into a very active ninth-grade social life. Ninth grade is the toughest year to negotiate, a transitional year, a time that falls between still being a kid and becoming a teenager. Passing puberty, racing toward *Go*. Sometimes we call ninth grade the end of middle school—the last year of junior high—and sometimes we call it freshman year of high school, nothing junior about it. Which is how Sydel sees ninth grade. No more junior high, no more kid's stuff. She has not entered high school casually, on tiptoes. She has burst into high school. Translation: fitting in, parties, boys.

She knows, though, that we have a family rule about all that. Same rule I instituted for her brothers, Stephen and Seth. Very explicit. Very clear. Uncompromising. No debate. A rule that can't be broken and one I enforce.

No dating until you turn sixteen.

In Sydel's case, no boyfriend.

Absolutely no boyfriend.

"So I wanted to talk to you," Sydel says.

Oh yes, she's got an agenda.

"About?" I say.

I brace myself for whatever she's got.

Okay, girl, I'm ready, bring it.

"Tomorrow night," she says.

"What about tomorrow night?"

"I think I've mentioned this to you before."

She halts, curls her lips slightly, shifts in her chair.

She has not mentioned this before, whatever *this* is, though I can guess.

"The *party*," she says, as casually as she can, as if she's discussed the party dozens of times. Then she powers past the details like they don't matter, irrelevant bits of meaningless information—time, place, the girl who's hosting.

"Actually," Sydel says, gesturing elaborately. "We're going to a movie first, then back to her house for, you know, the, uh, party."

She punctuates the word *party* with a dismissive wave. "Really just a few of us hanging out."

I feel myself nodding.

"Who are these friends?" I ask, stalling. "The ones attending this party?"

I know the answer. Sydel has recently been invited into a new social circle. This group has embraced her, the cool, status-y newcomer. The group consists of a few older kids, including one or two I've heard about through parents. These kids, I'm told, are a bit more—*mature.*

I also know that hovering around this group is a particular boy. A crush. Sydel doesn't talk about him much. But she talks about him enough. It's not how much she talks about him that matters. It's the way she does it. I have an intuition about these things. Boys. Matters of the heart. Crushes. I, too, raced past ninth grade. I see myself back then, a freshman in high school, no junior high about it.

"Sydel," I say, "you're fourteen."

"Going on fifteen."

"In a month."

"Twenty-eight days."

"But who's counting."

Sydel adjusts her position on the chair, tucks a leg beneath her.

"Please, Mom. I want to go. You know these kids. They're my friends—"

She lists them.

"So only girls?" I say. "You didn't mention any boys. No boys will be at the party?"

"Well, I mean, maybe, there could—"

I hold up my palm. A stop sign.

"Sydel," I say quietly. "I don't want to be the bad cop here, but you know the rule. No dating until you turn sixteen—"

"This is not a date. It's a party. A get-together."

"Sydel," I say, sharper.

"Mom."

Another adjustment in her chair and in her tone.

"Everybody's going," she says.

I hate that argument. *The everybody is doing it* defense. She knows I hate it. But it's her last gasp—her Hail Mary pass. She has no other option. She has to go for it.

"Please," she says.

I wrap it all up for her. My summation.

"*Sydelllll,*" I say, drawing out her name to make a point, then allowing it to land heavily, all without raising my voice. "I don't feel comfortable about this. You are fourteen years old. You are not sixteen. And I know about the boy situation. I want to remind you. We have a rule. You know very well what it is. I'm going to have to say no. I'm sorry."

That's it. The end.

Except it's not the end.

Sydel keeps going. She keeps fighting, flailing. She raises her voice. She blows by logic now and goes straight for emotion.

"I don't *understand.* Why can't I go? It's a *movie* and then because it'll be so early, a few of us are getting together at a person's house whom you *know.* A few kids. That's all it is."

"I'm sorry," I say again, closing the conversation. "You're not going to go."

She purses her lips as if she's swallowed something sour and then she says, flatly, "You are the worst mother in the world."

I feel my throat constrict.

Time stops.

You are the worst mother in the world.

I cannot believe these words have spewed from my daughter's mouth.

Not from Sydel.

Then I feel myself doing it—the *Oh, no, you didn't* neck and eye roll. The look my mother, Candy Adams, gave me whenever I crossed the line. The look every Black mother on earth shoots at her child whenever they cross the line. The neck and eye roll just comes out of me. A reflex. An instinct. I can't help myself. Here it comes. I'm giving my daughter the Candy look.

That sentence. Those eight words. Parents at the school and friends who are parents have told me that their kids have hurled this sentence at them. This dagger. When they told me, I thought, *I can't imagine my kids ever saying that to me. No. My kids would never say that to me.*

But my daughter has said it. The sentence I consider my worst nightmare.

You are the worst mother in the world.

I have worked so hard at being a good mother. I wake up every morning, gearing myself up for the day, for this role—mother. I define myself as a mother. It is more than a definition. It is my essence.

Sydel has crushed me. She has cut me to my core.

Then I stop myself.

Hold up. She has said those words to me over not going to a PARTY?

I sit up straight, my back as erect as a dancer's.

"Okay," I say, my voice sounding thin and distant. "I've heard what you said to me loud and clear."

I pause now. Sydel squirms. She sees that she has hurt me, but she doesn't know how deeply the wound has penetrated.

"Sydel, based on what you just said, I want you to go upstairs and think about those words. *Really* think about them. And while you're thinking about what you said to me, I want you to think about who you want to live with—*instead of me.*"

She stares at me, immobilized.

"Consider that very carefully, Sydel. After you do that, I want you to tell me who I should call to ask if you can live with them. I'm not going to put you out of the house and on the street. I wouldn't do that. But since I'm such a bad mother, I'm going to give you the opportunity to go live in a household with someone you respect more and who you think will be a better mother to you than I am. I will give you one hour to make your decision."

She stares at me for what feels like a full thirty seconds. Her eyes study me, measure me. She knows that I don't bluff. I don't say things I don't mean. I don't threaten—I promise. She knows that I am telling her to make a decision. Does she want to live in this house, with me as her mother, and abide by our rules, or does she want to move out? Her eyes glisten. Again, I read her thoughts— *Does she mean this? She can't mean this. Can she?* And then I read her hesitation, followed by her realization—*She does mean it. She really is giving me this choice. To live here or move out.*

Sydel pushes herself away from the table, hops off the chair, storms out of the kitchen, and thunders upstairs to her room.

I gasp.

What have I done? Have I gone too far? What if she decides to move out?

"Sonya," I murmur. "I can't believe what you just did."

Then I wonder if I'm in some kind of dream. I pinch my arm to be sure. I shudder. Then I look up at the ceiling and say, "Did that just happen?"

The empty chair across from me and the even deeper silence that descends tell me that it did.

But this is a different kind of silence. This silence feels ominous. Momentous. Even dangerous.

My hand starts to tremble.

I reach for my phone and call a friend who has three daughters. She answers right away. My voice shaking, I describe my exchange with Sydel. My friend, who knows me well, listens. As I speak, I hear her breathing intensify.

"She knows I was serious," I say. "Serious as a heart attack. I meant it."

"You always follow through," my friend says. "I admire that."

We both go quiet.

"Are you waiting for my approval?" my friend asks. "You want me to tell you that you did the right thing?"

"I don't know. Probably."

"Sonya, you're her mother. You make the rules. This is your decision. This is not for me to judge whether it was the right thing to do."

"I was kind of hoping you would."

We both laugh, then after a pause, I say, "Was I too hard on her?"

"Again. Not for me to say."

I lean onto an elbow and start to talk softly into the phone. I sniffle and feel a tear slide down my cheek.

"You know my struggle with Sydel. You know that I don't feel as if I'm a good 'girl' mother. I always worry about that."

"I know."

My head starts to throb. I rub my forehead.

"Maybe I'm not listening to her. I probably need to listen more. Do you think I'm listening to her?"

"Sonya, you do listen to her," my friend says. "Ninth grade is a tough transition."

"That is true."

"One more thing. You are a *great* mother."

"Not according to Sydel."

"Well, we hurt the ones we love. And we all have doubts. I certainly do."

"I consider you a wonderful mother," I say. "In fact, you're so good, in about thirty minutes, you may have another child."

My friend laughs at the absurdity. After a moment, I join her, laughing to let off steam.

"Seriously," I say, "she might come downstairs and tell me she's going to live in your house. She might pick you."

"Let's see," my friend says, unwilling or unable to say anything more.

"It would break my heart," I say softly, and then we end our call.

For a moment, I stay frozen at the kitchen table, my phone resting in my open palm. A few minutes ago, I sought out the silence in this house. Now the silence feels as if it might choke me. I hold my hand in front of me and watch my fingers shake.

The worst mother in the world.

How do I heal that wound?

Then I ask myself, *Will Sydel decide to move out?*

I wait a few more minutes, check the time, sigh massively, and then I call to Sydel. I ask her to come downstairs.

Silence.

Again.

Then I hear her footsteps.

No urgency this time. A tentative padding, moving slowly down the stairs, step by step.

Will she have her backpack slung over her shoulder?

Will she be carrying a suitcase?

She hits the landing at the bottom of the stairs and comes into the kitchen. No backpack. No suitcase.

"Well," I say. "What's your decision?"

She shifts her weight. She keeps her eyes fixed on the floor. She won't look at me. She can't look at me.

She's going to leave. She's not going to live here anymore.

She raises her eyes to meet mine.

She speaks in a tiny, wounded voice.

"I want to stay here," she says, her eyes filling up. "I can't believe you would actually put me out."

"Oh, babe, I will never put you out. I was just letting you know that if I'm such a bad mom, you deserve someone better. You do not deserve to live with a bad person. If you really, absolutely think I'm that horrible, you are blessed enough to have other people in your life who would take you in and treat you the way you want to be treated—and deserve to be treated."

"I don't want to live anywhere else."

I grab her in my arms, tight, and while neither of us are major huggers, this time we hug it out.

In midhug, I say, "Sydel, promise me—"

"I know, Mom, I know."

"I can never hear those words come out of your mouth ever again.

Because it's all about the words you say. Always. The words you say are powerful. More than that. Those words are forever."

"I promise."

"Good. Thank you."

"You know I didn't mean it, right?"

I nod, feeling my eyes fill up.

Silence follows. I feel then that something has changed between us—within us. I think about Sydel differently.

My baby has started to become a young woman.

2

Teaching Philip to Read

SUMMER 1976.

I am ten years old. We live in a trailer park. Rows of rectangles. Lines of boxes. Mobile homes. An oxymoron. A home should be a place where you settle. Where you stay put. Something with a foundation. Not mobile. Not a home on the move. That's exactly how I feel, too. Fidgety. Wanting to *move*. And yet, as restless as I feel, we don't move. We stay right here. In our rectangle. In our line. In our box.

My mother has remarried. She and her husband—my stepfather—have three kids together, my two stepsisters and stepbrother. I am the oldest and the only one who has a different biological father. Even after my stepfather adopts me, I still feel like an outsider. I feel as if I don't fit.

I move in with Granny Evelyn, my maternal grandmother. Granny has an extra bed. It is in her room, but I don't care. I have a bed all to myself. My mother's trailer is cramped, noisy, and chaotic. Granny and I both crave quiet. She seems to thrive on silence.

Granny is soft-spoken, serious, and so fair-skinned she looks white. She has gray eyes and coal black hair until it turns completely silver. Granny never raises her voice but always makes her point. When she expresses an opinion or offers an objection or criticism, her volume stays level, but her intensity rises so dramatically it sends you backward, like a slap.

My mother, Candy Adams, is a quarter Cherokee. She's dark-skinned with long black hair, and she too parses out her words carefully. But unlike Granny Evelyn, my mother laces her infrequent words with cutting humor. Candy grew up in a segregated section of Radford, Virginia, and was part of the first class to integrate Radford High School. The school mascot was a Confederate Rebel. She dealt with prejudice every day. People said ugly things on a good day. The rest of the time she had to fight. She went to school prepared to fight every single day.

Candy is funny and tough. All my friends want to hang out with her. She is the neighborhood draw. The favorite mom. She's hilarious and gangster. Nobody messes with Candy.

She is also sensitive and caring. She listens to you, really listens, and then when you don't expect it, hits you with words of wisdom, or concern, often along with something bitingly funny. Everyone thinks of her as a badass, in a good way.

Sometimes we go to Rocky Mount, an hour and a half away, and visit my adopted father's relatives, a very religious, apostolic family. They attend church several times a week and live by very traditional, old-school rules. Basically, the men work and the women stay home. This results in a clear separation between them. I feel thrown off by this. I like to hang out with guys, but in Rocky Mount, as opposed to my life in Radford, the women stay in their group while the men stick together.

The Rocky Mount family also adheres to a dress code. Women—including girls my age—can't wear pants or jeans. Females wear long skirts or dresses. No shorts. I can't do that. In the stifling Virginia summers, I wear shorts. I can't help it. I may be visiting Rocky Mount, but I live in Radford.

And in Rocky Mount, girls don't play sports. That's a no-no. I don't conform to that rule, either. I play sports as well as most boys. No, I don't fit in here, not with this side of the family.

I will say, though, that I find myself gravitating to one aspect of my adoptive father's strict, churchgoing family. The rules. They have a lot of rules. While I may not agree with or follow all of them, I like the idea of having rules. I know where I stand when I go to Rocky Mount. And within the structure of these rules, I feel safe. *Rules work*, I think.

I decide to start my own school.

I'm ten. Old enough. Throughout the school year, I have collected homework sheets, pieces of chalk, art supplies, and a few books. When summer starts, I gather four or five younger kids who live in the trailer park. They're happy to enroll in my school. Their parents are even happier. They see my school as summer camp and they see me as the head counselor, or more accurately, babysitter. I don't care what they call me. I call myself a teacher.

I turn my tiny bedroom into a classroom. I sit the kids on my bunk bed, set up a small table for their desk, and begin the day's lessons. I turn the wood paneling on the closet door into a blackboard. I write spelling words and arithmetic on it with chalk and allow the kids to write on it, too. I pass out ditto sheets and pencils and crayons and give them assignments and art projects. I keep a schedule for the whole school day. I allow the kids recess, provide a snack—crackers and cups of water—and I give homework. The kids treat me like a real teacher. They raise their hands in class, fill out their ditto sheets carefully, and hand in their homework on time. Of course, I give them grades—all As. I'm a strict teacher and an easy grader.

During the summer, I become friendly with Philip, a tall, shy eighteen-year-old who lives near the trailer park. People say Philip has mental issues. *Slow*, folks call him. I see him as kind of quiet, friendly, and a gentle soul. Whenever I bump into him, I smile and say hello. Philip always returns my smile with a warm, wide grin.

Philip begins hanging around our trailer, his head lowered, rarely speaking. I invite him to sit on our steps and offer him a drink. One night, I ask my mother about him. She calls Philip "special." She says that Philip seems to like me, but he feels uncomfortable around most people, probably because he's illiterate. She thinks it makes him feel inferior. I decide that I will teach Philip to read.

One day, I sit next to him on our steps. I bring out a pad and paper and I start writing out the alphabet. I sound out each letter, taking my time, and then I ask Philip to repeat everything I say. When he gets frustrated and wants to quit, I don't let him. I keep at him. I admit it, I can be a little bossy. He does what I say, as carefully and enthusiastically as the kids in my "class." Sometimes, Philip gets confused when I show him that a letter has more than one sound, like "o," which has a long "oh" sound and a short "ah" sound. I don't rush him. We take our time. I try making my teaching a game and sometimes we laugh. Every day, around the same time, Philip comes over to our trailer, takes his spot on our steps, and we begin our reading lesson.

Finally, one day, he grasps the entire alphabet, and we move on to a *Dick and Jane* reader that I've borrowed from school. We page through the book, then I read it to him. I point to the drawing on the first page that shows Dick and Jane's dog, Spot. I point at the sentence, "Run, Spot, run!"

"Rrr," Philip says, sounding out the letter.

"Good, Philip."

"Ra."

"You got it. Keep going."

Philip puckers his lips, then shakes his head.

"Come on, Philip," I say, quietly. "You can do it."

I refuse to let him quit. I won't let him give up.

"You're going to get this," I say. "I believe in you."

He tilts his head, then turns back to the book, and squints at the page.

"Ru—*n*," he says.

"Yes. Great. Keep going."

"Spo."

"Short *o*," I say.

"Spah."

"Yep. And—"

"Tuh."

He looks up at me.

"Spot," he says.

Then, peering at the page, Philip says, "Run. Spot. Run."

"Philip." I slap the step next to me. "You *read* that."

He nods, bites his lip.

"You read your first sentence."

I nudge him with my shoulder.

"You can read. Philip, you can *read*."

He lowers his head. When he raises his eyes, I see that they have filled with tears.

I grin. He chokes back more tears, and then I say, "Come on, man, you got a whole book to read to me. Let's do this."

As Philip turns to the next page and begins sounding out the next sentence, I think, *Sonya, someday you're going to be a teacher.*

3

I Think I Killed Him

WHEN I am eleven or twelve, my family—aunts, cousins, and a few close friends—forms an all-female softball team. We are formidable. Our entire family is athletic. People call us Radford's "first family of sports." I am too young to play softball, but I love to watch, and the team makes me the official scorekeeper. My mom can hit. The team becomes a big part of our social lives, and because we are so good, we feel the enormous sense of pride and accomplishment that comes with winning.

We win our league and earn a spot in the championship game that will crown the softball queens of Radford, playing for the city title against an all-white team. As our team warms up on the field, I get ready to keep score. The umpire calls, "Play ball!" Our team starts to take their positions when a loud crash that sounds like thunder cracks through the humid afternoon. I look up. In the distance, I see a Ku Klux Klansman riding on a white horse, strutting on the crest of a hill, his white sheet billowing. A cross he has planted in the ground behind him smokes and burns. The horse prances, the white-robed rider's silhouette outlined in the flames from the cross, a frightening vision of hate.

"He trying to scare us?" someone on our team says.

His presence ignites a corresponding sense of anger and hatred in the other team. They begin shouting and pointing at us, and then they come at us. I put down the scorebook, turn to find my mother, and nearly get trampled by our entire team, grabbing their bats, heading toward the pitcher's mound to confront our opponents, the white team, who are waving their bats. All hell breaks loose. A brawl. Fists flying. Bats swinging. Women throwing each other to the ground. I feel myself spinning in a circle, trying to locate my mother, seeing her in the center of the melee, directing our short-stop to help our fallen left fielder, then leading the fight, mixing it up, her fist connecting with a face.

In a matter of minutes, we have won the fight, and the Klansman rides away. The teams return to their respective dugouts, and a few minutes later we start playing the game. We win the fight; we win the game, too.

"They thought we were going to run," my mother says to me on the way home. "Nope. We pulled up on them, kicked their butts, and the Klan guy ran."

I look up, see her smile, feel her pride.

Badass, I think.

One night, with my mother at work, my sisters and brother huddled in a corner of the kitchen, the cold outside whipping through the trailer park and seeping through our thin walls, the only heat coming from the oven that I've turned on, I say to myself, *We're poor.*

Of course, I've realized this before, usually when staring into our buzzing and barren refrigerator, but I've never permitted myself to formulate those words and allowed them to sink in. As I prepare dinner for the four of us—gravy slathered over bread—I answer the statement softly, but aloud, "You can fix being poor. And when I get older, I will."

I don't dwell on being poor. I try not even to think about it. I refuse to allow our lack of consistent cash flow to define me, even though, feeling embarrassed, I avoid inviting my schoolfriends over to the trailer park to play. Instead, I focus on staying on the move. That means basketball, volleyball, and track—any sport where I get to run. Athletes populate our family, so I see myself following in that family tradition. I'm especially drawn to my cousin Brenda, a few years older, who's my role model. Brenda has just begun high school and plans to take advantage of her athletic ability and earn a scholarship to college. I have a long way to go, but I vow to take the same path.

On weekends and summer afternoons, practically the entire extended family accompanies Cousin Brenda in a caravan of cars to her basketball games. At her games, we cluster in a group, taking up several rows of bleachers in whatever high school gym she's playing in, cheering for Brenda at the top of our lungs. Sometimes it seems our family makes up more than half the crowd. Brenda's team wins and wins—the league championship, the district championship, the *state* championship. *I want to do that*, I think. *I want to be on a championship team. I want to hold up a trophy, standing in the center of our team.*

I want to be the best—just like my cousin Brenda.

I play in an all-girls basketball league at the Radford Recreation Center. Our team wins every game and, modestly, I have a lot to do with that. I'm our point guard and one of the two best players in the league. I score most of our team's points, steal the ball anytime I want, and I'm faster than anyone who tries to guard me. I also work my butt off, hustling on every play. But our league has a "fairness" rule, or at least that's how I describe it, sarcastically. If I score too many points or make too many steals, the coach has to take me out of the game, to make the game "fair." I don't understand. I'm getting penalized for scoring too many points? I get benched for being—too good? This makes no sense. When I have kids, I vow to never penalize them for success. I will teach them to be humble, to appreciate their success. I'll also teach them to be confident and walk with their heads held high. Right now, I sit on the bench, watching our team play horribly—feeling ridiculous, frustrated—not understanding this stupid rule at all.

In addition to playing organized sports, I hang out at a local park and playground and play pickup ball—with boys. At first, they want nothing to do with me, but after they watch me shooting around on my own between their games, they decide to include me. Soon, I'm playing both basketball and softball with boys. I'm as good as most of the best players, better than some. Nobody really says anything about me being a girl, which is fine with me. I'm a good player, period. One of them. I feel accepted and respected. Plus, hanging out with boys all the time, I have an opportunity to do a little subtle flirting with the cute ones.

One day, as I start walking home from playing softball in the park, my baseball bat resting on my shoulder, a kid named Henry begins following me—and taunting me. He jabbers nonstop. Somehow, I manage to shut out his exact words. I drown him out, hearing only the drone of his constant yipping and yapping, a grating noise that bites into me. I keep trying to ignore him, hoping he'll stop, but my silence only makes him bolder. He keeps following me and— *yapping*.

I can't take it anymore. I whirl on him. "Henry, you need to stop running your mouth."

"Oh, yeah?"

"Yeah. I mean it."

"What are you going to do about it, girl?"

He starts taunting me again. I slam my mouth shut, turn away from him, keep walking. At one point, I actually put my hands over my ears, or try to. I can't really cover my ears and hold my bat at the same time.

Henry keeps coming—yipping, yapping, running his mouth— until I break into a sprint. I know he can't catch me. I race home, thinking that Henry has had his fun, that he won't bother me tomorrow.

He does.

Yapping, taunting, making fun of me.

Again, I try to talk to him. I reason with him. I tell him to stop.

We get into a back-and-forth conversation, which roars into an escalating argument. I tell him to stop, he tells me he won't, he keeps taunting me, I keep warning him. We're getting nowhere and I'm getting frustrated.

He does it a third day. He dogs me all the way from the baseball field to my street. I argue with him, asking him to stop, until I finally give up and again run away from him. This time, I nearly crash into my mother who has been watching me and Henry for about five minutes. She stands with her arms folded.

"What was that?"

"That Henry keeps running his mouth at me."

"I saw."

"He does it every day."

"Let me tell you something," she says, lowering her voice.

That's a bad sign. That means she's angry. She's about to deliver a direct message. Her badass is about to come out. I know what that means. Candy will go off. That means a whupping. Or when you least expect it, she'll grab the closest object to her—a wooden spoon, say, a box of something, or most likely a shoe—and throw it at you hard, hitting you upside your head. You never know exactly when she'll gun the thing at you, but you know it's coming.

"If you don't stop running your mouth back and take *action*, then you are going to have to answer to me. We don't start things. We finish them. Are we clear?"

"Yes, Mom," I say. "Crystal clear."

That night, I lie in bed and go over my mother's warning. I don't know it then, but her words will stick with me; they'll change me. From that moment to this day, I cannot abide back-and-forth bantering. It leads nowhere. I take a different approach. First, I go silent. I calm myself. Then I think things through. And then I act. Thinking about Henry, I consider why I have continued to argue with him. Maybe I hadn't wanted to jeopardize being invited to play with the boys. I reject that idea. I've established myself. Then I hear my mother's quiet menacing voice. Her ultimatum pierces me. The fear of Candy freezes me. But I know she's right. I'm through arguing with him. I will give him one more chance. If he doesn't stop running his mouth, I will take action.

For some reason, I half expect him to leave me alone after the next game because I don't see him at first. But when I start walking

home, he appears, raising his taunting to an even louder, more ob-
noxious level.

"Henry," I say, gritting my teeth. "I've been asking you for days.
Please stop running your mouth. Now, for the last time, I'm asking
you to stop. Or else."

"Or else *what*, baby girl? You're not going to do anything
about it."

I don't think. I don't plan. I don't even really *see*.

I grip my baseball bat, turn, swing, and connect the bat with
Henry's head. He crumples and folds onto the pavement like a rag
doll.

I panic.

I race home, breaking every speed record known to humankind.
I crash into our kitchen, lean on the table, breathless, panting. I exhale massively and my breath bursts from me, billowing gusts large
enough to blow a hole through the wall. I try to speak, can't. I'm too
exhausted from my sprint. Then I catch my breath and catch my
mother's eye.

My mother stares at me. "What's the matter?"

"I did it," I say. "I did what you told me."

I smile, hoping she'll be proud of me.

"Did what?"

"That Henry was running his mouth again, so I—"

I can't finish the sentence. Suddenly fear envelops me. I imagine
the police arriving at our door any minute, slapping handcuffs on
my wrists, hauling me off to prison.

"I hit him with the bat," I say. "I asked him to stop. He wouldn't.
So I hit him."

"That's good. You took action. Like I told you."

"I think I killed him."

She pauses.

"I bet he won't mouth off at you anymore."

"No, he probably won't—because he's *dead*."

We look at each other for half a second, and then a tiny grin sneaks across her face.

"Okay," she says, low. "Now you sit down while I go see what you did. I got to assess the damage." She shakes her head slowly. "Dang, girl. You didn't have to crack him in the *head*."

I look up at her "What if I did kill him?"

"Then who's the badass?" she says.

I see Henry the next day. He survived my blow to his head, but I left a mark—a nasty-looking purple lump.

He never runs his mouth at me again. And I notice from then on, nobody else does, either.

4

The River

EVERY SUNDAY, we go to church. Our whole family attends, from the oldest, my grandmother, to the youngest, my cousins who still sleep in a crib. We never miss. We wouldn't think of it. We go to church on Sunday morning. That's what we do. It's a part of our week. No questions asked. No excuses. It doesn't matter what you do the other six days, Monday through Saturday. Come Sunday, we get up, put on our good clothes, and head to church. To this day, I still hear Granny Evelyn's words ringing in my head, "You are waking up Sunday and you are going to church."

And if on a particular week, the church offers an additional, special activity, we participate—picnics, dinners, raffles, bake sales, food or clothing drives, handing out toys to toddlers at Christmas—we do it. We are in the middle of it all. We are more than churchgoers. We are church *doers*.

At twelve, I begin confirmation class. I have no choice. It's what you do. So, in addition to attending church on Sunday, I go to church with my friends a couple of times a week after school to learn about the fundamentals of religion. At the end of the year, confirmation class will culminate with a ceremony. Our pastor will take our class to the banks of the New River that flows alongside the town of Radford, and he will baptize us.

The school year begins. I dutifully attend church and confirmation class. But as fall sets in, the days turn colder and winter looms, I start asking questions. Not aloud. Not to anyone. To myself. I see and hear about members of the congregation—even members of my family—acting inappropriately during the week. They drink alcohol; some even get drunk. They go to parties and play cards. I call this having fun. The church calls this sinning. I'm torn. Do I want to commit to giving all this up at age twelve? I don't think I'm ready. And what if I become baptized and I can't help myself? What if I sin? I don't want to fail at being a Christian. I think of two Scriptures we studied in confirmation class. From James 1:22: "But be doers of the word, and not hearers only, deceiving yourselves." To me that means that you can't only listen to the word. You have to do what the word says. Otherwise, you're deceiving yourself.

I also remember Revelation 3:15–16: "I know your deeds, that you are neither cold nor hot. I wish you were either one or the other! So, because you are lukewarm—neither hot nor cold—I am about to spit you out of my mouth!" I understand. I can't just follow blindly like the other kids in my class. I have to feel it.

I don't think I do. I believe that if I don't really feel it—if I'm only going through the motions because that's what is expected of me—I won't be able to keep my commitment. That feels worse.

On occasion, I go to services at the holiness church my adopted father's family attends practically every day. These services scare me. I see people speaking in tongues and the pastor shouting at the rest of us, "You need to get saved right now! Because you could walk out that door and be hit by a car and if you haven't been saved—*you are going to hell!*"

I don't want to go to hell—I don't think I deserve *that*—but this pastor and his message fill me with fear. I'm confused. I'm frightened. I don't know what to think. I'm even starting to wonder what I believe.

A week before my baptism, I pray for clarity. I don't really know what to ask for—an answer, I guess—but I wake up the next morning knowing what I have to do. I will not be baptized. As soon as I come to that decision—to that realization—another kind of fear overtakes me. I'm afraid of breaking the news to my mother. I don't plan anything to say to her. I don't prepare an argument or a defense. I allow her lesson with Henry to be my guide. Even though I fear what my mother will say, I take action.

"Mom," I say, two days before I'm supposed to go down to the New River with my confirmation class, "I'm not getting baptized."

"What? Why not?"

"I don't want to. I don't feel it."

My mother pauses for an eternity and then she finally says, "Well, you better go tell your grandmother."

This I hadn't expected. I had expected my mother to lose it. I had not expected her to make me face my grandmother, the matriarch, the one who demands I attend church every week, without fail.

I approach Granny Evelyn the next day. For a moment, I can't even find my voice. Finally, I exhale deeply to calm myself, and I say, "Granny, I don't want to get baptized."

She leans back in her chair and traces me with her eyes. "Oh?"

"Yes. I'm not going down to the river. I'm not getting baptized."

Granny Evelyn stares at me. She seems to cinch up her face.

"Okay," she says.

That's all she says. She doesn't ask why. She doesn't argue. She doesn't try to convince me. What's more, when I leave, I know that nothing has changed between us. She has accepted my decision. She has accepted *me*.

If she had asked me why, I know what I would have said. I had rehearsed the reason. I had chosen the words carefully, not because they were in any way false, but because they were, in every way, true.

Sonya, I expected her to say, *why don't you want to get baptized?*

Because, Granny, I'm not ready to not do what I want to do.

At that moment—having just turned thirteen—I believed that Christianity would take the joy—the fun—out of my life. I didn't want that. I wouldn't accept that. I couldn't. Of course, later I would discover that's not what would happen at all.

I don't have to give Granny Evelyn the reason I won't get baptized, but if she ever presses me for a reason, I would turn to the Bible. I would paraphrase Revelation 3:15–16, "I'm not getting baptized, Granny, because I am neither hot nor cold, I am lukewarm."

5

Run

I RUN.

I enter Radford High School at full speed. I run so fast and so much that I barely stop to catch my breath. I keep my legs pumping. I keep moving. I never rest.

I come in as an athlete and I not only keep going, I up my game. I run faster.

Beginning as a freshman, I spend every season playing a sport— volleyball in the fall, basketball in the winter, track in the spring.

It's not enough. I want more. I decide to try out for the band. I don't play an instrument but that doesn't stop me. I want to high-step and twirl a flag. Actually, I don't really want to do that. I want to *try out* to be a high-stepper and a flag-twirler. I want to see if I can make it. That's my overriding goal—to see if I can make the team. I do it. I make it into the band. As soon as I get word that I've made it, I quit. I've completed my task. Done. No need to prove myself further.

I do the same with cheerleading. I try out for the squad and get picked. My volleyball coach gets wind of this and pulls me aside before practice.

"I heard you made the cheerleading squad," he says.

"I did," I say, smiling.

"Great. Small problem. Cheerleading conflicts with volleyball."

"Oh. Okay. I'll quit cheerleading tomorrow. I wanted to see if I could make the team."

After that, I decide not to try out for any more teams—until my friends who are runners beg me to go out for the cross-country team so we can hang out while we do our five-mile training runs.

So, for them, I try out for the cross-country team. I meet the coach and the other long-distance runners the next morning at six a.m. I run stride for stride with my friends. After another five-mile run the next day, the coach informs me that I've made the team. He tells me that my first official practice as a member of the team will be six a.m. the next morning.

"How many practices do we have at six a.m.?" I ask.

"All of them," the coach says.

None for me, I say to myself, right before I tell the coach I've decided to quit.

I want to challenge myself. I want to see if I'm good enough to make all these other varsity teams, ones that may be out of my comfort zone. I don't really want to play two sports at once or play one sport and be a cheerleader for another. The truth is I hate being bored. I have to keep myself occupied. I need to be on the move. I need to run.

My mother rents an apartment not far from my grandmother so I leave Granny Evelyn's and move back in with my mom and siblings.

But I spend very little time at home. I'm almost always at school either practicing or playing games, or on the road, hanging out on the team bus with my friends. I love being on a team. Even better—I'm on a good team. During my four years of high school, we win two state championships in basketball and two in volleyball. I also do well in track—both on and off the field.

Toward the end of junior year, an older gentleman shows an interest in me. Meaning—he flirts with me. I'm sixteen, going on seventeen. "Rick" is twenty-one. At first, I find his interest flattering. As time goes on, I find myself battered by a wave of contradictory emotions. I feel special that Rick has chosen me. I like the attention. And I wish he would leave me alone.

I feel attracted to him. And I feel embarrassed that I'm attracted to him. I feel pressured by him. I hate being put in this position. I know what I'm feeling is wrong. I don't act on these temptations, but I can't help what I feel. All these contradictions weigh on me. I'm a good kid. I play by the rules. I always have. I used to pretend to be a *teacher*. But now, when I'm with Rick, I want to be a rebel. Mostly, though, I feel confused and alone.

In my heart—and in my mind—I know what I should do. I shouldn't see Rick at all.

I'm not that strong. Or I'm too caught up in the idea of having a twenty-one-year-old boyfriend. An older man. An authority figure. A white man. In Radford, Blacks and whites don't mix. All this adds up to something—forbidden.

I'm drawn to the *idea* of him, this older, attractive white man. I know that. Rick makes *me* feel attractive. He's answered the questions every sixteen-year-old girl asks herself: Will boys find me pretty? Desirable? Will I ever land a boyfriend? Not only have I found a boyfriend, I've got me a man. I've hit a home run my first time at bat. I feel so validated. At the same time, I know I'm in over my head. I want someone to tell me what to do. I need someone to help me.

I need to tell my mother.

I'm afraid to tell my mother.

Candy will go off, I know that.

So I don't tell her. I keep Rick a secret. As I begin senior year, I find myself slipping. I know I'm falling into a bad place with Rick. I know I shouldn't be involved with him. I know I should extricate myself from this relationship, but I don't know how. I'm so confused. I don't know if that's what I want. I don't know what I want.

I need to tell my mother.

I'm afraid to tell my mother.

One day, after seeing Rick, I sit by myself in the bleachers, feeling so alone and so lost and so ashamed that I decide to tell my mother. I realize that I don't just want to tell her, I want her to handle this. I need my mother to deal with the mess I've gotten myself into, to clean it up. I'll take the consequences. I don't care. I need her help. But I am afraid to tell her.

Turns out, I don't have to tell her.

I don't know how she finds out, but it couldn't have been too hard. We live in a small town and news—especially gossip—travels. She hears about Rick and me through Radford's small buzzing grapevine.

That night, my mother confronts me about Rick. I'm halfway glad and somewhat relieved to have this conversation. I want her to take action.

My mother hears me out. She nods as I talk. I can see her taking in everything I say. Digesting my words. When I finish, I sit quietly, waiting for the backlash, waiting for the badass to come out. Finally, she speaks.

"I don't like it," she says.

I drop my head, preparing for the explosion, waiting for her to go ballistic.

The explosion never comes.

Instead, she says quietly, "I don't want you seeing him anymore."

That's all she says. She gets up from the kitchen table where we've been sitting. She has ended the conversation.

That's it?

I want her to do more. She hasn't given me a whupping in years. I began our conversation half expecting her to grab me and give me one now. I would have been shocked, but I wouldn't have been surprised. *That's what I would have done to my kid*, I think.

At the very least, I expected her to lose it. If not a whupping, I figured she'd ground me for the rest of high school. But she leaves it at that.

"I don't want you seeing him anymore."

I want more fire. More fury.

Do I want her to threaten him? Go to the school? The head coach? The principal? The police?

Maybe.

I don't know.

She seems too calm, too complacent, too controlled.

I want to see some typical Candy.

I want to see some badass.

At that instant, something stirs within me. I experience a kind of epiphany. In my confused, troubled, and terrified state, I actually envision what *I* will do as a parent.

First and foremost, I will pay attention. I will plug into my children. I will not allow something like this situation with Rick to happen with any of my kids, especially if I have a daughter. I will be vigilant to a fault. I don't care if my kids hate me. I will not allow my kids to be put into this same kind of position.

How?

I will create strict boundaries. I will establish curfews and enforce rules for dating—for my kids and for anyone they see. If anybody they go out with dares cross those boundaries, I will step in with a vengeance. The person who crosses those boundaries will have to deal with *me*. Right now, I am seventeen years old, in way over my head with Rick, and, at best, an apprentice badass. But when I have children of my own, I will step in. Yes, one way or another, I *will* step in, and the badass will come out.

Bless my children's hearts.

After I talk with my mom, something strange happens.

Rick becomes cool to me at school. Distant. Icy. Outside of school, he's suddenly very busy, forgetting to tell me about commitments he's made with his family or friends. He's clearly avoiding me. I feel annoyed at first, even hurt, and I back off. I wonder if he's found somebody else. Then my competitiveness kicks in and even though my mother has told me not to see him, I do. I sneak out and meet him, and after a while, he breaks down and we see each other on the sly. Sneaking around makes seeing him even more exciting. Instead of seeing him less, I probably see Rick more.

After a while, I find out why Rick gave me that initial cold shoulder. My mother sent him a message, delivered by at least two of her larger male relatives: "Stay away from Sonya."

Fearing for his health, Rick decided to listen to them.

He hadn't counted on me sneaking around to see him.

I can't resist temptation and neither can he.

We continue to see each other all through senior year.

Radford being that small town, I'm sure my mother knows.

Years later, with Rick a distant memory, I ask her why she didn't step in again and even stronger.

"I couldn't stop you," she says. "I knew you would sneak out and see him. I was resigned to it."

She shakes her head. "Sometimes God lets you do what you're going to do so you can learn the lesson on your own. The hard way."

Ultimately, I deal with Rick on my own.

It happens in college. I don't have the courage to do anything about our relationship while I'm in high school. I need the advantage of being away from Radford. To act, I need distance. And I need to be in college. In my mind, that gives me credibility and confidence and, in a way, power.

In my family, I am the first woman of my generation to go to college. In addition, I am the first to be *paid* to go to college. I enter Virginia Tech on a Pell Grant plus a scholarship to play volleyball. Once I get to Blacksburg—twenty minutes up the road from Radford—I settle in my dorm, a brand-new horseshoe-shaped facility built to house athletes, women on one side, men on the other. I love being on my own, creating my schedule, enjoying my freedom.

Rick, though, doesn't want me to have any freedom. He wants to possess me. He wants me to be his wife. I remember an unsettling incident in high school. One day, I spend a few hours at his place doing homework while he runs errands. He walks in, looks around, and says, "Where's my lunch?"

I'm so thrown, I only manage to say, "Huh?"

Thoughts—emotions—crash in my head.

You expect me to make you lunch? *That's an outrageous expectation. What year is this? We're not married. Fix your own lunch.*

I suddenly look into my future.

Is this what I want?

Is this where I want to be, what I want to do—and who I want to do it with?

No. No. And *no.*

I don't make his lunch, but I feel afraid—not of him, but of being unable to express what I really feel. I realize that in this relationship, I'm starting to lose sight of *me.*

Soon after I arrive in Blacksburg, Rick starts hounding me. He calls me constantly, insisting that he visit me and spend the weekend. I put him off as long as possible. I love being at college, living in a dorm, being on my own. But there's Rick, persisting, calling, pressuring me, a harsh reminder of home. I don't know what to do. The old feelings rise up. Rick's so different and that's part of the attraction. He's older, confident, bordering on cocky. I don't know if I want to show him off to my friends or show him out the door. Finally, weakening, I agree to let him come to Blacksburg for a visit. Am I making a big mistake? Or am I finally giving myself the opportunity I need to end our relationship?

The moment he arrives, I feel unsettled. I decide to give him a chance, or at least the best chance I can. I show him the campus, introduce him to friends, and at night, we go to a party. He feels out of place here, uncomfortable, and so do I. After a while, he suggests we leave, go for a drive. We cruise around a bit, and then he finds a remote spot off-campus and pulls over. He doesn't waste time. He gets aggressive and then he starts getting sexual. I stop him.

"Rick, no."

"What?"

"I'm not doing this."

He loses it. "You always say that. You know what? We've been together for two years. I think we should—"

He paws me again.

I pull away. "Stop it."

He grabs my arm. "You listen to me. You're going to be my wife."

I look at him and my eyes glaze over. At that moment, I decide to embrace my fear. The instant I do, I feel the courage come. I decide I'm going to choose what I want rather than give in to what he needs.

"No," I say. "This is not happening."

"What do you mean?"

"This. Us. It's over. Take me back to my dorm."

In a quiet rage, he moves away from me. In silence, we drive back to my dorm. I sit pressed against the window. Rick seethes, leaning over the steering wheel, glaring into the night. He pulls up in front of my dorm. I think I say, "Goodbye, Rick," as I close the car door. I hear him drive away behind me, the tires screeching. I don't turn around. As I walk into my dorm, I don't know if I actually said "goodbye" aloud, but I know he's heard me. I have taken action. I have ended the relationship on my own turf, on my own terms. I feel free.

6

Choice

A FEW weeks later, I meet Dell Curry.

We literally bump into each other.

I open the door to exit our dorm at the same moment he opens the door on the other side to come in. Our eyes meet, but we don't speak. I look at him and do a double take. I recognize him. I've seen him before. But where?

It takes a second and then I remember. I saw his picture in a program my mother brought home from a Virginia Tech basketball game she attended. The moment comes back to me, clearly. A Sunday afternoon. Two years ago. I am a junior in high school. I sit at the kitchen table, passing time, flipping through a schoolbook, chilling. My mom stands at the stove across from me. I see the glossy program on the table and I pick it up. I leaf through it, look at the players' photos. I stop and stare at Dell Curry, Virginia Tech's star player.

"Wow," I say. "He's cute."

"Who?" my mother says, stirring a pot.

"This guy. Dell Curry. You know something?"

"What's that?"

I pat Dell's face on the program. "This is the kind of guy I want to marry."

I see Dell again a few days later at volleyball practice. The men's basketball team and the women's volleyball team share a practice facility, two gyms side by side. During a break, I walk to the water fountain in the hallway outside the gym. I bend to take a drink and as I finish and straighten up, I glance into the men's gym and I see him again. The guy from the game program. Dell Curry. He's practicing with the team. I give him more than a passing glance. I give him a lingering look. I'm not going to say I'm checking him out. Okay. Fine. I'm checking him out.

Sometime later, Dell tells me that one of his coaches encouraged him to check *me* out.

"Who is she?" Dell asks.

"A freshman volleyball player."

"A *freshman*?"

He must get past the stigma associated with my being a freshman because Dell and a few other basketball players attend an upcoming volleyball match. After the game, we all head back to our dorm. Dell and I split off from the pack of players and find ourselves walking together.

"I'm Dell," he says at one point.

"I know," I say. "I'm Sonya."

"I know," he says.

After a while, Dell and I start hanging out, and I find myself pulled into a whirlwind of college life—seeing Dell, playing volleyball, attending classes, studying, partying. Time devours me. In a blink, a semester passes, and Dell and I remain, still standing in the center of that maelstrom. I don't think Dell's friends, team-mates, or even his coaches thought that he, a Big Man on Campus, would give this lowly freshman a second look. Then—blink—I'm no longer a freshman. I enter sophomore year, and then second semester, Dell, a senior, is named Player of the Year in the Metro Conference, and the Utah Jazz pick him #15 in the first round of the 1986 NBA Draft.

Utah, I think. That feels so far, so foreign. I imagine a grid of tall, modern buildings clumped inside a basin surrounded by stark red mountains. Something out of a science fiction movie. A city grow-ing on the surface of the moon.

"The Utah Jazz," Dell says.

"Let's enjoy the summer," I say, wondering if these three months will constitute the end of our relationship.

Life slows to a crawl that summer, with Dell and I trying to see each other every second we can. Time ticks by as if in slow motion. As the sweltering heat of August envelops us like a heavy coat, Dell leaves for Salt Lake City, and I start my junior year. We see each other sporadically—Thanksgiving in Utah, at home for the All-Star Break, a weekend in Atlanta. I finish my junior year and Dell comes back to Blacksburg in 1987 for the summer. Then over the summer, I bring him some unexpected news.

I'm pregnant.

We sit in Dell's car in the parking lot outside Planned Parenthood in Richmond. We have traveled nearly four hours from Blacksburg. I have spent most of the ride either asleep or in silence, escaping, I guess. We sit in the car now, waiting, because we're twenty minutes early for my appointment. For my procedure.

I don't want to go in yet. To be honest, I'm not sure if I want to go in at all. I haven't said that to Dell. On the entire four-hour drive, I haven't said much of anything. Thoughts have been flying around in my head, whipping by, and I have not been able to catch any of them. Dell, quiet by nature, has gone even more quiet on this drive. Practically the only sounds on the drive have been the hum of the car, the rumble of the road, and Dell softly munching on sunflower seeds. As we sit here, parked outside the clinic, a mix of contradictory thoughts and feelings collide.

Starting with—crushing disappointment. I have been raised in the church. I have tried to live by my faith, attempting to be obedient, thinking of others first, the good girl. Now, here I am, pregnant—for the second time. Nearly a year ago, on a cold, rainy fall day, my roommate and I drove to a different Planned Parenthood, in Roanoke. I told Dell after the fact. I remember almost nothing of that day, except my feelings of angst and shame. Now, pregnant again, those feelings return. I've messed up again. I have let myself down. I want to ask for God's forgiveness, but I really need His help. Curled up in the front seat, tucked in tight to the passenger-side door, I'm too ashamed to ask for that.

Do I really want another abortion? But do I really have a choice? *You're still in college, Sonya,* I think. *You have one year to go. You want to finish.* I always finish what I start. I want to get my degree. I *need* to get my degree. I want to be a teacher. How will I manage that with a baby? Having a baby will completely destroy my plan.

I look at Dell. He shifts his lanky body and drapes his long arms over the steering wheel, munching the sunflower seeds, his eyes narrowed, peering through the windshield. He seems lost in his own world.

What about Dell—and me? Where are we going with this? We've had fun, we're an item, but are we a couple? Are we a—*we*? It's one thing to be a couple, quite another to be a family. Is he ready for this? Does he want this? Will we get engaged and get married? Or have we reached the end? Our end.

And there's the matter of our parents. My mother has no idea I'm pregnant. I try to imagine telling her. She is going to flip out. More than ever, I fear the wrath of Candy. I shudder, imagine hearing her voice: "You made your bed, now lie in it!" followed by a sharp, daggerlike stare at Dell, "Are you going to take care of my *daughter*?" And what about his parents? Will they think I've "trapped" him? *College Junior Ensnares NBA Player.* We've seen that movie before, too many times. That story has become so common that the NBA has started to give classes to rookies about the perils of getting involved with women—groupies, in some cases—who go after players, actually trying to get themselves pregnant, and then taken care of, financially.

That's not my story. Not even close. I will never force Dell into anything. Of course, because we've never had a serious, in-depth conversation about our future, I don't really know where we stand.

I take a deep breath, glance at Dell, then check the time. Ten minutes before my appointment.

Do I want to go through with this? Do I want to go on with my life?

Or do I want to change my life?

A baby.

Having a child.

The idea scares the crap out of me.

For so many reasons.

First—commitment. I am literally putting a person's life in my hands. The decision to have a child seems—is—monumental. I wish that every mom would take a breath, slow down, and at the very least, go through the process of thinking about having a baby, starting with, *Am I ready for this commitment?* That doesn't begin to cover it. Having a child is not merely a commitment. It's a commitment unlike any other. You can get out of any other commitment. You can never end your commitment once you have a child, no matter how old a child gets.

Second—confidence. I have always wanted to have children. I believe that's part of my destiny—to be a mom. I want to be a mom. I almost feel as if I were meant to be a mom. But to be a mom, you need to have confidence that you will not screw your kids up. I do have that confidence, that belief in myself. I know I can do it. I believe you have to enter motherhood with more than a little confidence. You need a swagger. You even have to take on the body language of swagger, including some quiet power in your voice. You have to say without saying—*I got this.* I see a connection to sports in every aspect of my life, including being a mother. To be a mom, I believe you have to wake up every morning and put on your game face. *Let's do this. I am ready . . . no matter what happens.* There exists no more crucial career.

Third—money. To be a mom, you have to make a financial commitment. Kids cost money. They just do. And more than young moms realize. You need to make providing for your child part of your decision. I learned a lot from my upbringing. We struggled, but we made do. I know this: I will give my child more than my mother was able to afford. I'm in college, a year from graduating, from completing my degree, for that very reason—to get a job and begin a career that will provide financial stability for me and my child's future.

I check the time again.

Five minutes until my appointment.

What should I do?

Dell shifts his position in the driver's seat. He, too, checks the time and then slowly turns toward me.

"Well," he says. "Are you sure you want to do this?"

I look at him. "Are you sure you want to do this?"

He takes a long pause and then he says, "It's up to you."

I look out the window. I follow the row of rolling hills in the distance. My eyes travel to the ground between the hills, patches of green nestled between pockmarks of dug-out brown dirt. I squint at the tops of the trees beyond, twigs pointing into the sky like spires. The day has turned cloudy, humid, sticky. I turn back to Dell. I speak so quietly that I can barely hear my own voice.

"Dell," I say, "I don't want to do this again."

He nods almost imperceptibly.

"Then you should have the baby."

"Are you sure? I don't want to put any pressure on you. I don't want to put any pressure on *us*."

"No pressure. I'll be there."

I don't say anything for a long time. I'm trying to gather my thoughts and look into my future at the same time.

"What do you think about me going to Utah with you?"

"I mean, I love you, so that would be fine."

Not exactly a marriage proposal, but I consider his words to be as close to a commitment as Dell is able to give.

"I don't want to force you into anything," I say.

"You're not."

I want to say more, but I can't. I just know that in this moment, everything has changed. In a blip, I have gone from deciding whether to maintain my current life to committing myself to a whole new life—with a child.

And then there were three.

What if this—Dell and I—doesn't work out? I think.

What if I end up having this child on my own? Do I have the strength and courage and fearlessness to make it as a single mom?

I shudder, shake off that vision of my uncertain future, and focus on the present.

"What about our parents?"

Dell shrugs. "We'll just tell them."

"That's it?"

"Yeah." He pops a fistful of fresh sunflower seeds into his mouth and shifts the car into reverse. "We're done here."

It hits me driving out of Richmond.

I'm going to have a baby.

"Wow," I say. "This is serious."

The silence returns. Soon, a new emotion snakes into my mind. Fear.

"My mother," I say. "She is going to kill me."

I look over at Dell. He sits poised over the steering wheel, driving with concentration, intensity, his forehead furrowed.

"I think I'm freaking out," I say.

I feel my head starting to droop. Sleep begins to come on again.

"I'm having a baby," I say, dreamily.

"You're having a *baby*?" my mother says.

"Uh-huh," I say, because that's the only expression—the only sound—I can muster.

My mother eyes me, then shakes her head, slowly.

"I was waiting on the moment when y'all was going to come and tell me this."

"You're not—"

"Surprised? No. It was just a matter of time." She faces Dell, clamps her lips shut, and takes him in. She nods. Then she speaks in a low voice, a soft growl.

"You are going to take care of my daughter."

Not a question.

"Yes."

She nods again. "You better."

Dell's dad smiles when Dell tells him the news. His mom cries. I'm not surprised at either reaction. His dad has always been, like him, measured, quiet, stoical. His mom knows what having a baby means. With modest means, she raised five children— four daughters and Dell, the youngest—in a two-bedroom house.

"Old school," Dell said to me about his upbringing. "Tough times."

"It's hard to raise kids," his mom says now. I imagine she's recalling the challenges she faced as a mom.

"Bottom line," Dell's dad says. "It's your decision."

"We're going to do it," Dell says.

"Well, then," his dad says. "Make sure you take care of everything, son." He considers me, then faces Dell. "And make sure you take care of her. Do the right thing, Dell."

"I will," Dell says.

It doesn't take me long to pack up and say my goodbyes to my friends, my family, my aunts, and Granny. Dell and I find an apartment in Salt Lake City, and I enroll at the University of Utah for my senior year. *I will finish my degree,* I tell myself. The thought nags at me. It becomes my mission. I know that I can be a mother *and* a teacher. Working will fulfill me as a person and make me a better mother. I believe that.

Shortly before I leave Virginia Tech, I meet with my volleyball coach. I tell him that I am pregnant and that I'll be going to Utah with Dell. His reaction throws me.

"Sonya, please don't leave school," he says. "Even though you're pregnant, you can help with the volleyball team. Stay here. I really don't think you should go."

"Wow. I did not expect you to say that."

"I've gotten to know you pretty well," he says. "You don't quit. You don't give up."

"I'm not quitting. I'm going to have this child. I'm going to be with Dell and we're going to do this together."

"Okay," he says. "I just want to say one thing. Finish your degree. If you don't, you'll always regret it."

Cold.

That's how Utah feels.

Flat cold ground surrounded by rugged white-capped mountains. I find myself staring at those snowy peaks. Drawn to them. Trapped by them.

I feel a different kind of cold when I walk to my classes. Cold shoulders. Icy looks. Confused and then blank stares. People looking past me. I miss the warmth of Virginia. In every sense.

I really don't fit here. I feel alone. Isolated. I don't experience hostility. I experience exclusion. I understand why. Sheer numbers. Only 1 percent of the students at the University of Utah are Black. Translation: three hundred Black students out of thirty thousand. We are not a minority. We barely exist.

I walk through my days, attending classes, my body changing, my stomach growing, feeling even more out of place. I'm now a pregnant Black undergraduate. I wouldn't want to calculate that number out of thirty thousand. My original image of Salt Lake City—a picture I created—remains not only confirmed but stuck in my head. I feel as if I have landed in the middle of a distant, uncharted planet.

September passes. October arrives. The NBA season starts and Dell spends half his time on the road with the team. I try to adjust to his comings and goings. I love when he comes home from a road trip, but I know he's here temporarily. When he leaves, my loneliness intensifies.

One day, in mid-November, the end of the semester in sight, Dell comes home after practice with a shocking announcement.

"I've been traded," he says.

"What? Where are we going?"

"Cleveland."

"Wow. Well. Okay. We'll have to break the lease, pack everything up, I'll finish the semester. This could take a minute."

"Sonya, I'm leaving tonight."

"Tonight?"

"That's how it works in the NBA."

I don't remember much of the next few weeks. I have a foggy memory of finishing the semester, packing up the apartment, taking care of every detail of moving, while feeling sluggish, slower, bigger. And I remember that Dell and I become officially engaged in December.

Happy New Year, 1988.

Good morning, Cleveland.

I prepare for my last trimester of pregnancy. I settle into Cleveland, our neighborhood, make some friends. I don't miss Utah. The

Cleveland winter is no joke, but I find it much warmer than autumn in Salt Lake City.

On a chilly mid-March morning, I wake up early feeling strange. My entire body seems to be vibrating. My usual daily discomfort makes way for something else, a sensation I have never felt before. It takes me a moment to realize, *Sonya, this is it.*

I fumble for the phone and call the hotel where Dell and the team are staying in New York. The desk can't connect to him and I can't wait. I call my mom.

"I don't know what's happening," I say. "But I have an idea."

"Has your water broken?"

"No."

"Take a shower. If you don't feel better, call me back."

Even through the phone line, I can feel my mother gearing up for action. Candy in *go* mode.

I shower and I feel worse.

I call my mother back.

She tells me to get to the doctor.

Now.

I'm afraid to drive so I call a friend. I must scare her a little because she arrives at my door in what seems like ten seconds flat. Within minutes, we arrive at the doctor's office. He takes me right into his examining room.

"You're three centimeters dilated," he says. "Go to the hospital." He looks up and smiles. "You're having your baby today."

I leave the office and waddle as fast as I can to my friend's truck. Breathing hard, I roll inside, clutching my bag. I close the door and my friend floors it. She drives like a getaway driver to the emergency room entrance. I roll out of the truck and move as fast as I can to the receiving desk.

"Curry," I say, blurting my last name, panting as I speak. "I'm having a baby. You can probably tell."

"Curry." The admitting nurse frowns. "Curry?"

"Yes."

She peers up at me behind her computer screen. "You're not registered here."

"I have to be. I know I am."

"I'm sorry. We don't have anybody by that name —"

I start to lose it. "You have to be *kidding*. I know we registered here. Akron City Hospital."

"Oh," the admitting nurse says. "You're at Summa Health Akron is just a short—"

"I'm at the wrong hospital!" I shout, lumbering outside at a near sprint, finding my friend. I roll back into her truck. "Wrong hospital."

"Sonya," she says, looking into her rearview mirror. "A police car just pulled up beside us. What is going on?"

The police officer lowers his window.

"Follow me," he says.

My friend and I look at each other, stunned.

"Wow, police escort," I say. "Just like in the movies."

The police officer fires up his siren, pulls his car in front of us, and leads us to Akron City Hospital, only two blocks, but feeling like a million miles away.

The pain starts to engulf me. I make it to admitting, a nurse checks me in while another nurse lowers me into a wheelchair. We take the elevator to the maternity ward.

"We have no rooms available," a nurse tells me at the nurse's station. "You're going to have to wait out here in the hall until I find something."

The pain comes harder, faster. I breathe short, shallow breaths, trying to remember my exercises. The pain sears through me.

"I have to use the bathroom," I say.

In a fog, I start to enter the bathroom when another nurse intercepts me. "Hold on," she says. "You have to lie down. The doctor wants to see you."

"Where are the drugs?" I mutter.

Suddenly, my world seems to spin, and before I know it, someone guides me into a bed in what looks like a makeshift hospital room set up for the moment. It almost seems that they've rolled a hospital bed into a supply closet. Another wave of pain and then the doctor sails in and examines me and I hear him say, "Okay, Sonya, listen to me, you need to start pushing."

"What about drugs? I want the drugs."

"You are past the point of an epidural." The doctor speaks sharply to somebody else in the room. "We need a delivery room. Now."

I hear muffled voices: "Sorry," "Nope, none," "No available birthing rooms," and then I'm lowered onto a stretcher, and someone wheels me down a hallway and into a cold operating room, and again I hear the doctor's voice, one word, a command, the only sound in the room, the only sound in my universe.

"Push."

I do, with all my might, and then—a squawk, a cry, some rustling below me, and I am looking into the face of my son.

I stare, mesmerized.

He has a big head. Gorgeous, arresting eyes. I feel myself pulled into his face like a magnet. I recognize him. I have seen his face before.

"E.T.," I say. "He looks like E.T."

I look up at the doctor and a squadron of nurses who surround me and then I look back at my baby.

"You're beautiful," I say.

Then I lower my face into his and I whisper, "We made it, son. No help, no birthing room, no drugs. We did it ourselves, the two of us, just you and me. We did it."

March 14, 1988.

I give birth to the baby boy I almost didn't have.

We name him Wardell Stephen Curry II.

I call him Stephen.

7

To a Degree

MOM.

The enormity of the word dazzles me. The sheer joy of the word.
Mom.

It defines me.

I look at Stephen, a week old. Calm. Content. He gurgles, grins.
He seems so happy to be here. He's got the life. He eats. He snuggles.
He sleeps.

We spend all our time together. Mother and son. I watch him,
amazed at the miracle of what has just happened. I am the mother
of this tiny human. I feel powerful and indescribably humbled. I
walk with him, slowly, whispering to him, listening to him literally
come alive, and as I hold him, I realize that in a much deeper way,
he holds me.

When Stephen turns two weeks old, I take him to his first NBA
game. The Cavs are home to the Celtics. He sleeps in the car all
the way to the game. As I make our way to our seats in the arena,

he hardly stirs. He's conked out, his tiny nose scrunched, lost in a deep sleep. *This little dude sleeps a lot,* I think. I don't mind. In fact, I feel that he's taking it easy on me. He's so easy that I wouldn't mind giving him a little brother or sister to keep him company. If they're all this good, this calm, this *easy*? Why not go for another couple of kids? Well, anyway, that's my not-so-secret plan.

We take our seats in the arena. The teams run out of their respective locker rooms, onto the court. The crowd cheers. Folks in the stands around us shout, whistle, applaud, horns bleat, the buzzer sounds. And still Stephen sleeps.

The players gather at center court for the tip-off. They slap hands, crouch into position for the start of the game. The two centers jump and—

Stephen's eyes pop open.

He's become wide awake.

I don't know what he can see, but he stares toward the action of the game for the entire first quarter. He seems to follow the play at each end of the court, completely captivated. At one point, I take my eyes off the game and study Stephen. I know he's heard these sounds in utero from my being at other games, but—no, this is impossible—he seems to be *intently listening to the sounds of the game.* Focusing on the action. Concentrating.

The first quarter ends. The players huddle on the sidelines around their coaches. Then and only then does Stephen start to fuss. He's announcing that he's hungry. I take him to the back of the arena and feed him. He crashes, instantly falls asleep. In the middle of the second quarter, I take him back to our seats.

His eyes pop open.

He's again drawn to the action on the court and keeps listening to every play until the game ends. The game seems to hypnotize him, soothe him.

Twenty-five years later, sportswriters, fans, and basketball pundits will call Stephen a student of the game.

So true.

He started studying the game in my arms when he was two weeks old.

In June 1988, Dell gets word that we're leaving Cleveland. The Charlotte Hornets, one of the NBA's newly formed teams, have chosen him in the expansion draft.

We will move again—the third time in two years—this time to Charlotte, North Carolina.

We are going back south, moving two hours from my family.

In August, in my hometown of Radford, we get married.

Barely.

In my wedding gown, I stand frozen in the back room of the small church. I face the sanctuary. Through the closed door, I hear organ music playing as my bridesmaids walk down the aisle. In one minute, I will take that same walk. With "The Wedding March" playing joyfully at my back, I will arrive in front of the pastor and join my soon-to-be husband.

Except right now, I can't move.

It's so cold in here, I think.

I'm shivering. My legs and feet begin to quiver, and I realize—

I am having cold feet. Literally.

I force myself to inch toward the door, taking a tiny step toward my future, toward my marriage, and I stop. My legs have locked. I can't *move*.

I turn and see an open window in the back of the room.

An invitation? An escape? A way out?

I drop down to my knees.

I speak aloud.

"God, please, I'm asking You. Help me. I'm stuck. I don't know what to do. Tell me. Do You want me to go out that window or walk through that door?"

Silence.

I hear the opening notes of "The Wedding March."

My stomach clenches.

Tears stream down my face.

"Please, God. Please. Tell me what to do."

Someone knocks on the door.

The door opens a crack and my aunt Vicky—my mother's sister-in-law—eases into the room.

"Sonya," she says.

I turn toward my aunt. She is framed in the doorway. For one second, she seems outlined in light. She looks like an angel. A messenger.

"It's time," she says.

God has answered me. He's given me my answer. He has sent me my sign.

It's time.

I rise to my feet. I wipe my eyes, look at Aunt Vicky, and I nod.

"Okay," I say.

"You look so beautiful," Aunt Vicky says.

I look up, toward the heavens.

"Thank you," I say.

Two years later, in August 1990, I give birth to my son Seth Adham Curry, a calm, laid-back cuddler who loves to snuggle, and I love snuggling with him. Meanwhile, our family has done more than settle in Charlotte; we have found our home. I have found my place, where I want to live, and where I want my kids to grow up. Dell, quietly, has become a local celebrity. He has entered his third year of what will be a ten-year career playing for the Hornets. He will become their leading scorer, and then, after his retirement, he will join the broadcast booth.

But two years in, while I love living and raising my two boys in Charlotte, I feel restless in another way. The nagging feeling I've always had to complete my college degree has developed into something of an obsession. My old volleyball coach's words echo. I'm not a quitter. I don't give up. I need to finish what I start. I look at my transcript and determine that I still need thirty-seven credits to graduate. I meet with a counselor at the University of North Carolina at Charlotte to see if I can complete my degree there. I learn that UNCC won't accept all my credits from Virginia Tech. I will have to start over. After more research, I discover that the only way to complete my degree is to reenroll at Virginia Tech and finish my coursework there, in person, on campus.

That would be totally impractical.

No.

That would be insane.

"Even if you wanted to do it, how would that work?" Dell says.

"I'll find a place to stay," I say. "We'll rent a house."

"What about the kids?"

"I'll figure out childcare. My family will pitch in. Yours, too. Maybe your sister would be willing to help. You know what they say. It takes a village. In this case, it might take a small city, but I *will* figure it out."

Dell shakes his head. "I know this. Once you set your mind to something, it's a wrap."

I think it through. I try to focus only on the task in front of me—finishing my college degree. How would I pull that off? To make my life slightly easier and avoid spending weeks away from the kids doing student teaching, I decide to switch my major from elementary school education to family and child development, adding a bunch of sociology and human development courses. To complete my degree in a year, I will have to take eighteen credits my first semester and follow that with nineteen my second semester. I will arrive in Blacksburg with my two babies, three-year old Stephen and one-year-old Seth. I will have to balance going to class, studying, and raising the two boys. I'll be a mother and a student.

"Yeah, it would be completely insane," I say, a moment before I decide I'm going to do it.

Summer 1991 to spring 1992.

I can barely remember that year.

I look back at that time and all I see is a frenetic, filmy overlapping of events.

I see Dell's sister, Stephen, Seth, and me moving into a house we've rented from one of Dell's old coaches. I see myself tucking the kids into bed and then going to class or to the library or to study sessions. I see myself—twenty-five years old—driving my Mercedes onto campus, probably parking illegally, students gawking, grinning. I see myself sprinting into a classroom, cradling an armful of books. I see us all driving two and a half hours one way to Charlotte for the weekend, then seventy-two hours later, driving two and a half hours back to Blacksburg. I see Seth and Stephen laughing, getting

into everything, growing. I see Stephen dunking his puffy little basketball through his plastic toy hoop and Seth toddling after the ball
and throwing himself onto it. I see some parties, lots of laughter,
and I see intense studying. I see very little sleep. And then I see
the month of June appearing on a calendar somewhere and I am
walking in my cap and gown, smiling at the dean of our college as
she hands me my diploma. I don't see tears. I see triumph. Then,
afterward, I see myself in the middle of a huge blowout party inside and outside of someone's big old barn. I stand with a group of
my fellow graduates. We all eat off paper plates and talk about the
past year, a time I can hardly fathom.

"How did you do it, Sonya?" someone asks.

"I have no idea," I say. "I didn't think about it. I just did it. A day
at a time."

"You must've been so exhausted."

"Oh, I went way past exhausted."

I pause.

"I'll be honest. Whenever I got down, or felt overwhelmed, I
would think about single parents I'd heard about or saw on campus.
I'd think, 'They're working and they've got children. How do they
do that? I'm fortunate. I don't have financial concerns. I don't have
to juggle kids, work, and school. If these working moms and dads
can do it, I can do it.' I am so in awe of those men and women. They
motivated me. Plus—"

I look over at Dell and at Stephen and Seth who are playing near
him on the lawn outside the barn.

"I had to do this—for *me*," I say, with a ferocity I don't expect. "I
was going to take on this challenge, and I was going to finish. I had
no other option."

"You're a strong woman," a classmate says.

I look at her and the other young women who have formed our circle, proud college graduates, none of them athletes, none from privilege, but each a part of the support system that got me—got us—through this fleeting blur of a year.

"We all are," I say.

8

Who Does That?

AFTER GRADUATING in the spring of 1992, I return to Charlotte. I hardly take any time to settle in. I'm motivated to move on. I'm done being a student. I want to get back to *life*, as a mom, and then as a working mom. I believe that working enhances motherhood, supports it, and so I intend to get to work, to start a career. But first things first. I need to find a preschool for four-year-old Stephen.

In my opinion, Stephen, who is smart and social, needs to be around other kids in addition to his brother. I want to find a school that's nurturing and nearby. I don't have to look far. I speak to several moms I know who have enrolled their kids in a local church's preschool and they all seem happy. I visit the school and find the teachers and staff to be loving, helpful, and nurturing. When I add the Christian aspect, affirming the spiritual foundation that mirrors our home environment, I feel I've found the school for Stephen, so I enroll him.

A short time into the school year, I decide to pick up Stephen early one day. For some reason, this feels important to me. I can't articulate why I feel the need to make an impromptu visit to his classroom, but I walk in feeling almost pulled, as if I have been brought here, told to observe, to take a close-up look at where my son spends the bulk of his days.

I don't immediately see anything of concern. But as I walk farther into the classroom, I feel that there's something—off. I know this feeling. A nagging, too familiar, churning in my stomach.

Whoa, I think. *Uh-oh.*

Pay attention, Sonya.

I cruise slowly around the circumference of the classroom, trying to grasp more specifically what it is that I feel, trying to make my instinct concrete. The teachers are lovely and kind but as I look at the kids' work posted on the walls, I see a sameness. No individual expression. A lack of creativity. And then I see something that grips my heart.

I face a display of ice cream cones. Each cone has a child's name written on the bottom. Some cones have one scoop of ice cream, others two, or three, or four. A couple have five or six. More than a few cones have no scoops at all.

What do these ice cream scoops mean? What do they represent?

After a moment, I figure it out.

Each scoop of ice cream represents how high a child can count.

I scan the display and find Stephen's cone.

He has fifty scoops, by far the most in the class.

I'm not surprised. I know he can count to fifty, and even higher. I have been working with him at home.

Competitive athlete that I am, I first feel pride. Victory. *We've won.* My child has dominated his preschool classroom's counting contest.

You got to fifty? I think. *That's awesome. You go, Stephen!*

Then, almost instantly, my spirits sag. My feeling of pride turns to concern.

If Stephen is that far ahead of everyone else in his class, he is certainly not being stimulated or challenged. He needs to be around other kids who are at his level. Otherwise, he will stagnate, become bored.

I come to an instant decision.

It's time for him to move on.

As an educator—and Stephen's mother—I have to move him into a more challenging environment. I don't know where or what that will be, but I know it has to exist somewhere. I will not settle when it comes to his education.

Then something else happens.

I find myself staring at the cones that have no scoops at all.

I look at the names of those children.

I know how I felt when I saw fifty scoops towering above Stephen's cone.

How do those kids feel seeing their empty cones posted on the wall above their names? I am drawn into a sense of how disappointed they must feel. How inadequate.

Four years old and they have already been saddled with a measure of failure.

What can this display possibly teach them? How can it benefit them in any way?

I look at the children huddled on the rug facing their teacher as she reads to them. Some kids listen intently, but many seem bored, restless, their active minds elsewhere. Stephen picks at the rug, disengaged, not paying attention. I look at the other children around him and I wonder which ones have no scoops on their ice cream cones. I think about their parents, but especially their moms. What did they think when they saw their kids' ice cream cones without any scoops? How did they feel about their kids, about themselves? Did *they* feel like failures?

As an African American female, I know what it feels like to be constantly compared, invalidated, to not be celebrated. I know what it's like being told in so many ways, both subtle and direct, that you are *less than*.

Celebrate yourself. Don't compare yourself to anyone else. *Cherish who you are.*

I have to find a school that embraces those values.

I start asking around. I talk to friends, family, connections from college. As I think about a new school for Stephen, I picture myself as a ten-year-old playing "school" back in my trailer park. I see myself then, the strict, traditional teacher, writing on my closet wall in front of my "class." I ran a tight ship. I taught daily lessons and even gave out homework that I expected to be completed and returned the next day. I assume that's what I'm looking for now—a school that provides structure, organization, homework, classrooms with neat rows of desks, kids at attention, facing their caring but tough teacher.

Then a friend mentions Montessori.

"I've heard of that," I say. "Isn't that sort of, what, free-form?"

My friend describes a little bit of the Montessori philosophy—kids learning at their own pace, taking responsibility for themselves, different age groups mixed together, no desks, no textbooks.

"Visit a Montessori school," my friend says. "You'll see."

I do, but before I go, I read everything I can about Montessori.

One phrase, a philosophy, sticks with me: "Follow the child." Instead of imposing a specific teaching style, Montessori embraces each child's individuality, pace of learning and learning style, interests, personality, even quirks. As a teacher, the idea is to follow the child instead of forcing the child to follow you. Maria Montessori, the founder of Montessori, professed that if we observe and listen to our children, they will tell you everything you need to know about their development.

This intrigues me. I look up Montessori schools in our area, pick out the closest one, and arrange for a visit.

Walking through this classroom, I see a world of laughter, love, and learning. Three- and four-year-old children read and do addition and subtraction. I see older children interacting with younger kids. Everyone seems engaged, happy, and *learning*. On the walls, I see splashes of creativity, individual expression. I don't see a display of ice cream cones showing how high kids can count.

"These kids seem really smart," I say to the teacher. "What's the trick? You go and find a bunch of smart kids and bring them all in here?"

The teacher knows that I am both joking and impressed.

I leave, thinking—*This is too good to be true. I visited on a good day.*

I visit a second Montessori school. This time, I see a diverse group of twenty kids spread out on the floor, working like busy little bees. I feel a buzz of excitement, engagement, even joy. I come back again, this time with Dell. We watch the kids interacting. If possible, I'm even more impressed.

"This is really nice," Dell says. "What do you think? This is your area."

"I want to enroll Stephen," I say.

And that's how it begins—nearly three decades of my deep, personal involvement with Montessori schooling.

I see an almost immediate change in Stephen. He falls in love with school. A year passes. He turns five and with some skepticism I enroll Seth in the same class. Two different kids. Two completely different personalities and learning styles. I'm not sure how—and if—this will work.

It works beautifully. They love being in the same classroom, staying connected, but developing a separate group of friends, which I find healthy. I keep an eye on them, continue to be impressed by the work they bring home, and when I can, I volunteer at the school. I keep a close eye but I watch from a distance. In the meantime, I begin working in retail to keep myself busy and sane, if not fulfilled. Another year passes, and I get pregnant again.

One day, at pickup, Maura Leahy-Tucker, the owner of the school, approaches me. "Can I talk to you for a minute?"

My face falls. A knee-jerk reaction kicks in. "Oh no. What did my kids do?"

Maura laughs. "They're fine. It's nothing like that. Can you come to my office?"

I park the car and inform Stephen and Seth that I'll be with them in a few minutes. They're thrilled. They get to stay at school longer. *Unreal,* I think. *Nobody likes to stay at school longer.* They run off to be with their friends in aftercare and I move inside the building and poke my head inside Maura's office. She waves me in with a smile and points to a chair across from her. I sit, nervously. I feel as if I've been called to the principal's office, which, in a way, I have.

"I've been watching you," she says.

I must stare in shock because Maura bursts out laughing.

"That didn't sound right," she says in her Irish lilt. "But I have been. And I've been watching your children. I have to ask you. What's your background?"

"Well, I have a degree in family studies and child development."

"I thought so. Okay, here goes. Have you ever thought about getting into education?"

I'm stunned. I want to blurt out my entire history—how I started my degree in teaching, how I went on a four-year hiatus to have my kids and then went back to school with a baby and a toddler in tow, and somehow—I still don't know how—finished my degree. But I only manage to say, "Well, I mean, yes, I would, actually." I shift in my chair. I feel my heart racing. I peek skyward, consciously trying to catch God's eye.

I need to ask Him—*What's happening here?*

"I don't have any kind of plan, though," I say to Maura.

"What about this?" she says. "We're relocating the toddler through kindergarten satellite program. I need an administrator to run it."

"Wow."

"I know. I'm hitting you with this out of the blue. Here's even more. Would you consider being my partner?"

Then she looks up for a moment, drops her eyes back down, and looks at me with such warmth, I almost feel bathed in it.

"There's something about you," she says.

"I'm so flattered," I say. "Thank you. I'm not sure what to say."

Do it.

That's what I want to say.

Instead, I say, "I need to think about it."

"Of course. Take some time. Think about it. Please."

I stand abruptly.

"Again, thank you," I say.

"You would be so good," Maura says.

"I will think about it."

And I will pray about it, I think, with another peek upward.

"Just let me know," Maura says.

"You're really serious about this."

"Oh, definitely."

"Partners," I say.

Maura nods. "Partners."

Yes, I will pray about it.

I have been doing that a lot lately. Praying. Reading Scripture. Talking with God. Communing with God. Connecting with God. Or trying to.

Since returning to Charlotte, after a couple of years' hiatus, I have felt called back to the church. At first, I went out of obligation. It grew out of my method of parenting, which came from my instinct, from observation, and from a sense memory of how I must have assimilated the way my mother and grandmother parented me. They were strict, but they also parented through ritual.

In the same way, I have started parenting partly by relying on ritual and tradition. First and foremost, I believe that when you have children, you should take them to church. Teach them about God. It's what you do. How I was brought up. But with my kids, I actually feel something deeper. I feel as if I am being drawn back to my roots. I don't believe that it's simply what I should do. I feel that God—going to church—is something more. It's a pull. I *want* to go. It's not just tradition. I want to make churchgoing an active focus of our lives. I want to establish going to church as part of our family's routine. It's beyond important. It's a value I feel in my core. It's how I want to raise my children.

And so, every Sunday, I gather up Stephen and Seth, and we go. Sitting in church, flanked by my two boys, I feel the power and comfort of routine. I repeat the same action until it becomes habit. We rely on our rituals. I believe that. Then, after a short time, something subtle begins to happen. The ritual goes beyond a rote activity. I start to look forward to going. Sitting at the same spot every week. Greeting the same people. Reading and sharing the same prayers. Listening to the pastor's sermon. All this has its own power. Soon I realize that this routine has become my survival. Going to church on Sunday offers a kind of sanity, a safe haven from the week. Something I can count on. A refuge. The routine becomes its own reward.

In church, I look at Stephen and Seth, so young, so impressionable, and at this age, so squirmy. I smile at them and they smile back not knowing that I am training them, engulfing them in a sweet dose of spirituality that will last their lifetimes. At least I pray that it will.

As I remember Proverbs 22:6, "Train up a child in the way he should go, and when he is old, he will not depart from it."

I walk through our house at night. Sometimes I stop abruptly, drop to my knees, and pray. And sometimes I slow my walk so that I'm barely walking at all, and I talk to God. I talk to Him as I would a close and trusted friend.

"Wow," I say the night after I meet with Maura. "That came out of the blue. Completely floored me. Does she see something in me that I don't?"

I am filled with doubt and insecurity. Then I feel myself getting on my knees. I slam my eyes shut and I pray, "God, is this my time? Are you trying to lead me into something? Something I can't see? A whole new—I don't know what it is—but *something*?"

I stay in place, rocking slightly, my eyes still closed. Then I slowly stand and get back into bed. I fall into a deep sleep.

When I wake up, I know. I walk into school the next morning, and I tell Maura, "You got yourself a partner."

We open the satellite school in August 1994 when I am seven months pregnant. I work up until the day that I go into labor, in October, when I give birth to my daughter, Sydel Alicia Curry. I have felt nervous about having a girl. I grew up a tomboy and then an athlete. I played with boys and competed against boys. I know boys. I don't know how to raise a female. I'm not good with dresses and dolls and all those girly-type things. I know how to run and shoot a basketball and spike a volleyball. What am I going to do with a *girl*?

Then, from the second I look at my daughter, I know her. I *see* her. I can tell that she is feisty and fierce and takes after me. I nearly gasp. Because I have a gut feeling that she will be my biggest challenge and my best friend. Sometimes I think I can read her mind. The moment I bring her home Sydel delivers me a message. An edict. She wants to get busy and she wants me to keep busy. I take off two weeks and then I go back to work. I run back and forth from work to home and back to work. By early 1995, Sydel starts coming to work with me.

Now a mainstay on the Charlotte Hornets, Dell has signed a new contract. We buy land at Lake Norman, about thirty minutes outside of the city where we plan to build our dream house. We begin the painful, exhausting, frustrating process of permit pulling, architectural design, and beginning of construction. At one point, early in the process, overwhelmed by it all, I am gripped by a sudden, gut-wrenching realization. I have scouted the area for schools and I have not found what I need. One night, after swallowing a small sour dose of panic, I sit down with Dell after dinner.

"We have a problem," I say.

He exhales. He has come to learn that when I begin a conversation with those four words, he'd best pay serious attention.

"What is it?"

"There are no Montessori schools out here. I've checked. Done all the research. Not one within forty-five minutes."

He nods. I fold my hands and keep going.

"I want to keep the kids in Montessori. It's very, very important to me."

"I know it is," he says.

"So."

He waits.

"I'm going to start my own Montessori school."

"Your own—?" he says and skids to a stop.

He did not expect me to say that.

"School," I repeat. "I think I have found a nice spot. Twenty acres of beautiful country farmland. It has a house on the property already."

"Who does this?" he says. "Who starts a school?"

"Me."

"Sure, I guess," he says, knowing that I'm making an announcement. I will be doing this. I will be starting my own school. When I begin a task, I don't go in. I go all the way in. Head first.

Dell sighs, starts to turn away, assuming the conversation has ended. But he notices that I'm not moving.

"Is there something else?"

"Yeah," I say. "I'll need an investor."

9

Follow the Child

THE MISSION seems impossible.

Build paradise from scratch.

I read a quote once: "The difficult I do at once; the impossible takes a little longer."

I focus on moving the ball forward, little by little, inch by inch, but always *forward*. I break down this monumental undertaking into tiny pieces. A tenet of Montessori. The joy of figuring it out, bit by bit.

Of course, it helps that we start with a little piece of paradise as our foundation. Twenty acres of pristine farmland in Huntersville. We will preserve nature, the woods, the flowers—another pillar of Montessori. We will create a world for our kids that allows them to commune with the land, walk in nature, hike among the trees and flowers. The flowers on the land always seem in bloom, wild bouquets ready to be picked, brightening a room, or taken to the local weekend farmers' market. I gaze across our twenty acres and see a pasture of sunflowers, and beyond that, corridors of trees, that will shade and comfort our kids as they hike and explore.

The build-out happens as if by a miracle, guided by magic. In what seems like a blink, we have created the impossible. One day, it is done. I walk into the main building of a full-fledged school. My school. We call that first building the red house. Past that, in a common area, I will sit in my office, a spot where I can watch the kids coming and going. I want to see these little people at work and at play, which often amounts to the same thing. After that beginning, the school will grow each year, eventually sprawling over sixteen thousand square feet of building modules. Every inch of the place, inside and out, feels like home. That's no accident. That's by design. I want the kids—and teachers and staff—to feel as if they have come to a home away from home. I believe that parents are kids' first educators, so I insist on maintaining that flow, that feeling of home, here. I try to re-create the coziness of home—low, soft lighting, natural wood, plants everywhere, a reading area, a comfy child-size living room.

Spirituality remains an important pillar of the school. To connect to the kids, I include telling stories from the Bible on a regular basis. But I don't want the stories told in a straight, dry way. I encourage creativity. We tell our Bible stories using video, skits, music. When we go into chapel, we embrace all different ways of prayer and praising God. I believe that everyone has their own relationship with God. I believe that these relationships are, by definition, personal, different from mine, yours, or anyone else's. I emphasize that. I want the children to respect one another and express themselves without fear.

I encourage conversation, discussion, different interpretations.

As a rule, we will tell that week's Bible story and then ask each other what we call "wondering questions." For example, we may talk about Jesus getting out of the boat and walking on the water and then we wonder—

"What do you think the men in the boat felt when he got up and started walking on top of the water?"

The kids rush to answer, to engage, to *wonder*—

"It was a ghost!"

"It was a dream!"

"It was low tide!"

And even, the contrary opinion—

"There's no way a man walked on water!"

You learn through stories. You teach through stories. In our school, in our Bible study, I want to hear all interpretations, all points of view, pro, con, insistent, definite, unsure, or confused. I want the kids to question themselves and one another respectfully. I want them to be open and to know that there are no wrong answers. I want them to express their thoughts without fear. I want them to feel valued. I want them all to feel safe. I want them to feel at home.

We run into snags with building our house, hassle after hassle, and decide to stop construction. As we prepare to open the school, we move back to Charlotte. Depending on traffic, I will commute a minimum of forty-five minutes to school each morning and forty-five minutes back each afternoon.

I hadn't counted on a commute. The idea to build a school came out of necessity, from having no Montessori school near our new home in Lake Norman. Now, back in Charlotte, I face a crazy two hours in the car every day.

That first week, in a daze and running late, I hustle Stephen, starting our school at fourth grade, Seth, entering second grade, and Sydel, a toddler, into the car. I drive, tuning out the kids' low-level squabbling, focusing on the road. I don't say much during the forty-five minutes door-to-door. I think I'm in shock. How did my life go from having our house and our school within a few miles of each other to—*this*?

One day, in the car on the way home, something happens.

I settle in for the drive. I breathe, calm myself, and then I look at my kids. I do more than look. I take them in. I gulp them in like air. I suddenly ask myself, *Who else gets this gift of time together? Who else gets to do this?* I no longer feel hassled. I feel blessed.

I begin the drive home in what will become a daily routine I will treasure. Our time. Our special time. We don't talk much on these drives, but we do talk. Mostly we decompress, each in our way. When we talk, we talk about the day. We share funny incidents that occurred. We work out small problems. We plan our schedules—homework, chores, sports commitments. We almost always stop for a snack. If we don't, I make sure I bring snacks that we share in the car. We kid with one another and we laugh. And we listen to music. Always music. Often gospel. We sing along. Or we just lose ourselves inside the music, in the praise, in the joy, in the voices, in the rhythm. Mostly, we share the time together, filling that confined space with our combined energy and spirit. We fill that car with ourselves.

For ten years, I will make that drive to and from school with at least one of my kids. What I don't realize during that first commute is that the car ride will become the highlight of my day.

We share a home, we share our schooldays, and I feel blessed that we do. But once in a while, spending so much time together results in a combustion. I learn quickly that too much time together can equal *too much time together.* As Stephen and Seth grow, an inevitable competition sets in, resentment appears, and then, sometimes, an explosion.

A year after our commutes begin, Stephen, eleven, fifth grade, and Seth, nine, third grade, have entered a period of sometimes subtle, sometimes intense sibling rivalry. Dell and I have intervened, trying to inject calm and ingrain in them the idea that we need to learn to compete with ourselves rather than with others. A Montessori teaching. We emphasis process over competition, not an easy sell in a family of competitive athletes. *Do your best, be your best,* I hear myself say, continuously. *You are you. Don't compare.*

I want to confine disagreements and arguments to our home, but once or twice emotions spill over at school.

One day, Stephen and Seth go at it over a chair. Stephen asks Seth if he can use his chair to stand on to reach something on a high shelf. No, Seth says. It's my chair. Stephen persists, tells Seth he needs to use his chair. *No,* Seth says again, with even more insistence. Distracted by something, Seth turns away for an instant. Seizing the opportunity, Stephen grabs Seth's chair and stands on it. Seth turns back, sees Stephen standing on his chair, and pulls it out from under his brother. Stephen goes sprawling onto the floor and Seth jumps on top of him. They roll on the floor of the classroom flailing at each other until the teacher, my sister, breaks up the fight. She hauls them both to their feet, grabs each by an arm, and drags them to my office. She explains the incident. I call Dell at home.

"Come and get your boys," I say.

"Are they sick?"

"No. They're suspended. They were fighting in class. You have to take them home."

"Seriously? I have to drive all the way out there to bring our kids home from your school?"

"They broke the rules. No fighting. I will not tolerate that."

"Can't you leave them in the office and drive them home later at the usual time?"

"No. I'm sending them home now."

Dell grunts something I can't hear.

"They will not receive preferential treatment," I say. "They broke the rule about fighting. They're suspended for one day."

"He started it," either Stephen or Seth says.

"Make that two days," I say. "You want to go for three?"

"Sonya—" Dell starts to say.

"They'll be in the office," I say, ending the conversation.

"On my way," he says, resigned, annoyed.

I glare at my sons.

"Your father is on his way," I say. "And he's not happy."

10

The Big Machine

AFTER TWO boring, fidgety days at home, the boys call a truce, negotiate peace, murmur apologies, and, day three, return to school.
On the drive in, they retreat to their respective corners, solemn in
the silence. I'm fine with the quiet. Between our bustling household
and the constant cacophony of a typical school day, I find moments
of quiet to be a rare and precious commodity. I take them whenever
I can get them.

I drive, exhale, tap my fingers on the steering wheel. My mind
goes then to these three children in the car. I think about how we
share our lives, our space. And I think of parenting. What I do. How
I face each day, relying on both instinct and intention.

Truthfully, when I started parenting Stephen, I had no idea what
I was doing. I was young, a newlywed, he was unplanned, and I had
no plan for him. I spent my pregnancy on the move. Dell and I lived
in three different places during those nine months. We started in
the South, headed west to Utah, then moved to the Midwest, to

Cleveland. I had to adjust to different environments, lifestyles, climates, social situations. Sometimes I didn't know if I was coming or going. As I passed through my second trimester, and then entered my third, I bought a few parenting books, read a chapter here and there. But I had trouble concentrating. I felt unsettled.

Then Stephen arrived—gently, softly, joyfully. God gave him—and blessed us—with a cool, even-tempered disposition. He—and God—allowed me to breathe. I found to my amazement and relief that my life as a parent kind of flowed. I never felt anxious or rushed. I wanted to be a mom. I had made a commitment to parenthood and I was ready. I knew instinctively that I had to take my time, go moment to moment, not rush. After Stephen's birth, I kept repeating to myself, *Sonya, make sure you slow down, be deliberate, be focused. It'll be all right.*

And it was. Stephen's disposition gave me time to catch up, to plan, to formulate how I wanted to raise him and my future kids.

First and foremost, I was determined to raise them under the admonition of God. *He is in this,* I felt. A partner. A guide. I looked to Him, leaned on Him, listened to Him—and to my heart.

From day one, I made a vow to equip my children to walk in the fullness of their purpose, for whatever God has in store for them. I know that He has something in mind. I don't know what. My charge is to move them toward that unknown goal, to help them find that purpose.

Also, from day one, I have employed my skills, relying on what I learned from my college education and from Montessori. It all begins with a plain and simple philosophy.

Children are not miniature adults.

Every human being goes through the same developmental stages.

We have to respect those stages. I feel strongly that we have to nurture our children and not control them. But they are children. We have to honor them, gently guide them, and remember they need to be nurtured and that they are always, constantly growing.

I envision a child as an acorn seed that, as a parent, you need to tend. Eventually, the seed will blossom. Before you know it, the seed will grow into a strong, thriving tree. I believe that it's a parent's job to provide the environment and nourishment for that seed to flourish. How?

First, get out of their way.

Second, try not to mess them up.

Support them. Give them over to God. Pray that hope and faith will take over. Pray that their purpose will be revealed. But that's not my decision, not my choice. I will not steer my children toward any specific career, goal, or purpose. I will, hopefully, prepare them. I will train them to be caring, compassionate, loving, and God-fearing. If I can accomplish that—if I succeed in that basic training—then I know they will become successful human beings. How do I define success? Simply this: working to be the best of yourself every day. That's the goal of the training. You must try to give the best you can—each and every day. You can't take days off.

Pregnant with Seth, I found myself reading more parenting books and being open to what other parents say in my community, my church, even at my school. After Seth arrives, I find myself implementing some advice from books and from listening to people. But I cherry-pick. I also dismiss advice that I read or that other parents prescribe. I hear myself thinking, *I can't get behind that idea. That is your word and your truth, and it may work for you. I just can't do it. It wouldn't work for me and my family.* I also apply Scripture, specifically 1 Corinthians 10:23: "Everything is permissible, but not everything is beneficial."

From my background in sports and education, and thinking about Scripture, I know that children need structure. Rules. And with rules naturally come restrictions. Things you can and must do and things you cannot and must not do. I consider myself strict. I won't call myself a badass mom, the way some people saw my mother, but I will say I can be uncompromising. Again, that's how she—and my grandmother—raised me and how I intend to raise my children. If I come across as strict, so be it. I believe that children feel safe when they know what is expected of them, when they know the rules, and when they know, without a doubt, that those rules are real and serious and can't be broken. Strictness. Consistency. Follow-through. Children feel safe with that kind of structure— and they feel cared for.

I am a mom. It's who I am. It's what I do. Being a mom drives me. Defines me. I wake up every morning and face the day with that definition as my conscience, my motor. I have taken on this Mom role with 100 percent of my being. I accept—and want—full responsibility as a parent. This is on me. I take on this responsibility as my mission, with purpose, with action.

I wake up early, before anyone else in the house stirs. Then, every day, I close my eyes and recite the Lord's Prayer. After that, I lie in bed, take a deep breath, exhale slowly, and take another, longer cleansing breath. In that moment, I become my own private coach. I give myself a pep talk. I say, low, so only God can hear, "Come on, Sonya, you got this. It's *Go* time. It's time to parent."

Maybe the idea of sports has become ingrained too deeply within my heart and soul, but before I get out of bed, I put on a game face. I prepare to *bring it*. To be a parent—in my opinion, to parent well— you have to bring your "A" game. Parenting is strenuous. Draining. Exhausting mentally and physically. I find it similar to playing a sport at a high level. I approach parenting the same way I did when I played volleyball in college and the same way I see Dell approaching professional basketball. You always have to think *next play*. It's a term that athletes use. You've got to have a short memory. In the flow of a basketball game, you'll inevitably make a bad play—you'll miss a shot, throw an errant pass, turn the ball over, commit a dumb foul. You will make a mistake. It happens. Part of the game.

You cannot dwell on that mistake. You have to correct in the moment, adjust on the fly, change your attitude and your mindset instantaneously. In basketball and in parenting, things happen. Surprises. The unexpected. And those moments that don't turn out the way you planned or hoped for or even envisioned—those mistakes—influence other human beings. Your teammates.

Your kids.

Children absorb everything around them. They are keen observers and they are sponges. You, the parent, are in charge of their environment, their world. When you make a mistake, you need to adjust quickly. You acknowledge, correct, and move on. And know this. You will mess up. And inevitably, you will doubt yourself. Don't. Do not let the doubt win. Push forward. Keep moving. But keep moving in love. Allow yourself some grace. Try to take on that *next play* attitude. Tell yourself, *Okay, that's over. Now—next play*. Move on, as quickly as you can.

You cannot stay in that mistake. Guilt builds up, doubt seeps in, and you find yourself overcompensating. Mostly, you can't dwell on the mistake, or the responsibility will crush you.

Here's a secret.

No matter how many parenting books we read or how many self-help manuals we study, we are all parenting on the fly. Unlike sports, we have no practice sessions, no exhibition games. We don't have any game film to watch or break down. When you parent, it's always game time. And every game is the playoffs.

The Big Machine.

That's what I call our house, referring to the way everything and everyone functions—or at least, the way everything should function.

For the Big Machine to operate at maximum efficiency, without anything gumming up the gears, everybody has to do their part. At the beginning of each week, I set up a schedule and a list of jobs and responsibilities for the week. I call it our "responsibility chart." Each member of the family receives a specific responsibility. A chore. The chore remains that person's responsibility for the entire week. Then on Sunday night, we switch. The chores are simple but crucial to keeping the Big Machine humming along—doing the dishes, taking out the trash, doing the laundry. In addition to the household chores, everyone has to take care of their own personal responsibility, better known as homework. Stephen and Seth have some homework, including a half hour per day of reading for pleasure and they have begun playing on sports teams. Sydel is just two and will start her chores in a few years. For now, I list everyone's chore that week on a whiteboard in our kitchen. I don't write anyone's name. By their request, we go by colors. Sydel, ever fashionable, will change her color frequently until in middle or high school, when she finally settles on orange. Stephen chooses blue and keeps that color. Seth picks a deep red, or burgundy. Dell chooses turquoise, the color of the Charlotte Hornets, his team.

"I'm going with black," I say.

"That's not a color," Seth says.

"It's every color," I say. "All the colors put together. So, yes, that's my color. I'm going with black."

Scripture says that we must always put God first. So that's what I do. Another rule. Another responsibility. Another commitment. I start the day with God.

On school days, we all get up at six in the morning for family devotion. The kids set their own alarms, but I check on them to make sure they're awake. Then at various intervals, we stagger downstairs and sit at our large kitchen table, some of us half asleep, groggy, annoyed. I always arrive first, with Sydel. Stephen, perkier than anyone would believe, comes downstairs next. He's ready to participate, eager to please. Seth, barely communicative, arrives next, moving in near slow motion, often needing an extra nudge to get him out of bed. He clops down the stairs, yawning, sometimes theatrically, I think.

We begin the morning's devotion, reading a passage from the Bible, a new chapter each day. The group's participation varies. I can usually count on Stephen to be my co-leader, eager and enthusiastic. Seth will go silent or mumble. Sydel will giggle or at least feign interest. She likes being here with all of us. Of course, many mornings I realize that much of the time, they are all half asleep and want to be anywhere but here. Still, they do it. Not that they have a choice, but they *do* it. I stay focused, locked in. I am in playoff mode, wearing my game face. I truly believe that this ritual will have a long-lasting, maybe even a lifelong impact on my kids. I am completely committed to starting the day this way.

We end by holding hands and reciting a group prayer. Finally, I ask if anyone has a question or wants to say something. Going clockwise around the table, we respond by either speaking or squeezing each other's hands, indicating that the person doesn't want to speak.

Thinking about our morning ritual, I wonder if the prayers we read sink in or have any direct impact. I'm not sure it matters. What does matter is that we share this daily devotion, this commitment, this family time with God.

Once a week, we hold a family meeting.

I think of it as a planning session, a way for all of us to look ahead to the upcoming week. A sharing of our calendars. From Montessori, we've learned to hold weekly meetings and to work on organizing our schedules. Time management. We see that as one of the keys to success.

We begin each Sunday by going to a ten or eleven o'clock morning service, then we usually go to brunch, then return home for an afternoon of chilling, family time, hanging out together. Most Sundays, we set our family meeting before we go back to church for the six o'clock evening service.

We hold the meeting at the kitchen table or sometimes in the living room or family room. In the kitchen, I keep our big whiteboard, on which I keep a master calendar. In addition, everyone brings their own calendar or notebook and a pen or pencil. We talk through the week, discussing what we have lined up—Dell's travel, the kids' games, practices, school events, homework assignments, family commitments. I lead the meeting. I usually start with the times we'll be going to church.

"Wednesday night," I remind everyone. "Church. You should write that down so no one forgets. Then, of course, Sunday morning and evening services."

I mark the master calendar on the whiteboard while everyone scribbles their schedule into their calendars. If someone has a conflict or feels confused, I help organize their week and their time. After we discuss the week's events, we move on to chores. I remind everyone of their upcoming responsibilities. We always leave time at the end of the meeting for discussion.

"Does anybody have anything they want to bring up?"

If I see shrugs or hear silence, I ask, "What are you feeling? Anything you want to talk about? Anything going on at school? With a teacher? A coach?"

Usually, the conversation involves a scheduling conflict. Over time, one of the kids may bring up something personal. When that happens, I insist on talking with respect and love. If someone has a school issue, a problem with a friend or a coach, or even with one of us, we deal with it together, all of us, as a family. My intention—my hope—is that our family meetings become a safe place for free expression.

It seems to work. We give our opinions. Depending on the subject, the conversation turns lively or funny. Mostly, though, we plan and set up our week. As I watch the kids write or erase in their calendars, I think, *This is part of the training. Finding rituals. Routines. And then putting your responsibilities down in writing.*

In the end, the family meetings become less about the scheduling and planning of the week, and more about spending a set, scheduled time every week as a family.

One time, as head of school, I find myself in the middle of a debate in Charlotte about redrawing the school districts' lines that determine which school each student can attend. Some members of the school board and a large and vocal group of parents want to return to the idea of "neighborhood schools," a not-so-subtle euphemism meaning segregated schools. I decide I need to talk to the kids about this. I bring up the issue at our weekly family meeting. I believe in preparing my kids for real life. I always want them to have as much information as possible. I do not like the shock factor.

"You have to pay attention to language," I say. "This is important. You have to understand what some folks are saying and see what they are really meaning to do. Their intentions."

"What are the people trying to do in these neighborhoods?" one of the kids asks.

"They want to bring segregation back into our schools." I shake my head. "You might not see sheets on people's heads and burning crosses on lawns, but we have systemic racism in our world."

Sometimes, when I bring up a serious subject, I'll see the kids rolling their eyes, or getting fidgety. I can almost envision the word *Whatever* appearing above all of them in a group thought bubble. Not this time. This time, all three of them stare at me, their faces lined with concern.

"Are you serious?" Stephen says. "You think that kind of thing can come back?"

They look at me expectantly, their eyes wide in shock.

"It wasn't so long ago that your grandmother went to an all-Black school," I say. "Those schools were inferior to the white schools. They barely had enough supplies to go around. They didn't have new books. They got hand-me-down textbooks from the white public schools. This is your grandmother. Granny Candy. My mother. No. Not that long ago."

My words land.

"Look, we're blessed," I say. "We've had opportunities. But we can never take them for granted. Freedom, equality, respect—those things don't just happen. We have to work hard for them. And sometimes we have to fight for them. We always have to be vigilant and willing to fight for what's right."

"Granny Candy had to fight every day," Stephen says.

"It was a different time," I say.

"Not so different," Seth says.

I nod, taking this in, remembering.

They'll remember this. We remember our stories.

That's who we are.

Our stories.

The Big Machine hums.

Most of the time. Because most of the time, the kids complete their chores on schedule, without complaint. I see this as part of the training kicking in. I live by a tenet, incorporating a value we teach in Montessori, a philosophy of learning—of life—adapted from Lao Tzu, the founder of Taoism.

"Give a man a fish and you feed him for a week. Teach him to fish and you feed him for a lifetime."

We live by that at home. I make it the main doctrine of my parenting. When the kids ask me for help, I try to redirect them. I want them to take the initiative, to identify and solve the problem on their own.

"Okay," I'll say. "How can you find this out? Where would you get this information?"

I want them to figure it out by themselves. That way, I believe, they'll own it.

When Stephen turns ten, he becomes eligible for a new weekly chore: doing his laundry. I announce this assignment at our weekly family meeting.

"Happy birthday and congratulations," I say, writing the chore next to his blue color on the whiteboard. "Welcome to the first week of doing your own laundry."

He stares at the whiteboard, moves his eyes to me, then back to the whiteboard. I pick up a slight trace of panic. He writes the word *laundry* onto his calendar, then slumps in his chair and lightly taps his pencil onto the page. I can almost read his mind—*I won't worry about this until Saturday.*

Then Saturday comes.

Laundry day.

Sneaks up on you, I think. The week—like most weeks—blows by.

Saturday morning, I see Stephen in the kitchen.

"It's Saturday," I remind him. "Don't forget."

He looks at me, faking a confused stare.

"Time for you to start washing your clothes," I say.

"Oh, yeah," Stephen says. "Can you come show me?"

"Let's go into the laundry room," I say.

He follows me, walking tentatively. He comes up behind me, hands on his hips. I point to the washing machine.

"Right there," I say. "See that label? Read the directions pasted there. It's easy."

"Why do I need to read the directions when you're right here? Just tell me how to do it."

Montessori, I think. *It's about the process. Figuring it out by doing.*

"Mom, just tell me," Stephen repeats, almost in a whine.

Don't give him a fish. Teach him how to fish.

"You can do this," I say. "You're a good reader. It's very simple."

I pat his back and leave the laundry room.

He'll read it. He'll figure it out.

I bound upstairs, start working on my own chores for the day, collecting my laundry and starting to strip the bed. As I pull the sheets and pillowcases off the bed, I realize—I don't hear the sound of the washing machine. I hear silence.

I wait, strain to hear any sound from the laundry room.

Silence.

What is he doing down there? Has my little space cadet gotten distracted? I ball up the bedsheet and walk downstairs, making a little extra noise to alert Stephen that I'm on my way. I don't want to sneak up on him and startle him. When I poke my head into the laundry room, I see him standing in front of the washing machine, his shoulders slumped, his eyes filled with tears.

"My eyes are wet," he says. "I can't stop."

"What's the matter?" I ask.

"I don't know. It's so frustrating. I don't know what to do."

"Did you read the directions?"

"Yes. But I don't get it."

"Okay." I pause to collect myself. "Here's what we're going to do. I'm going to go through them with you, step by step, one line at a time. Okay?"

Stephen sniffs, nods.

"Let's break it down." I point at the directions. "Read the first line."

"Separate light-colored clothes from dark," he reads. "Lift lid and load washing machine."

"In order to get the clothes in, make sure you lift the lid," I say.

We both laugh.

"Okay, keep going," I say.

"Select load size," he reads and looks up at me, uncertain.

"What do you think? Small, medium, large?"

"I'll go with medium."

"I would, too."

He finishes reading the instructions, one line at a time. He loads the washing machine, adds detergent and fabric softener, sets the load size, temperature, and then starts the machine.

He exhales, smiles.

"I got it now," he says.

"See? There you go, son," I say, and give him a high five.

"Thanks, Mom."

As I sort my clothes, I second-guess myself, for a moment.

Dang, woman, I ask myself, *couldn't you have just started the machine for your kid?*

I dismiss that idea, come back to my Montessori teaching. I believe he had to learn the process himself. I walked him through it, but he read the directions himself. He owned it. *I taught him to fish.*

As the kids grow and become more inquisitive, I discover that "Go find the answer" becomes my favorite phrase.

"What does this mean?" Seth will say.

"Look it up," I will say.

And as Sydel gets older, she, too, will pepper me with that question: "What is this? How do I do this? I don't understand."

"Google it," I say.

Or as I may have said eons ago, "Look it up in an encyclopedia."

Time goes by. My kids become proactive, relying more and more on Google. I'm happy to pass the torch. As they grow, they become increasingly self-reliant. Then we add a new member to our family.

Siri.

They ask Siri everything from the capital of North Dakota to how to write a proper business letter to the recipe and ingredients you need to make an apple pie.

I just hope Siri knows what she's talking about.

11

Save Me

EARLY SPRING 1998.

Middle of the night.

I lie in bed. Alone. Dell is on the road.

I can't sleep. I haven't been sleeping. I toss, turn, strangle the sheets, free them, blink at the ceiling. A phrase dances through my head—

Birth of the New.

Those words keep appearing to me. The phrase flashing in my mind.

Where did it come from? What does it even mean?

I exhale as loud as a drowning woman.

Breathe, I tell myself.

What time is it?

Two? Three?

I don't dare look at the clock.

I cannot sleep.

I need to sleep.

Birth. Of. The. *New* . . .

Speed.

I love speed. I'm all about speed.

I run fast. I move fast. I drive my car fast.

I drive my motorcycle fast.

A black CVR 600. A "crotch rocker." The thrill of cold metal. A blur on the road. I straddle my bike and rev my engine.

It's night. Pitch black. I am alone. I wear a bikini. Over it I've slung on a slinky black robe. It's thin, short. You can see my bikini as I ride.

I ride so fast the wind whips my face. My robe flies behind me, flapping like flimsy dark wings.

I've strapped my laptop to the handlebars. I've secured it. It's locked in. Doesn't move. Its silver screen stares at me. Taunts me, then soothes me. When I look at it, I see my reflection. Then my face fades out.

I ride through my hometown, Radford, Virginia. I ride *fast*. I gun down the familiar streets. It's so late and so dark that I am alone on the roads. Nobody else is out. The town feels desolate. I feel my aloneness. It's as if I am the only person alive in the world.

I come to the bottom of a hill. I stop my bike and above me, on the crest of the hill, I face my old high school. Radford High. I look up at the school. It sits there, imposing, high above me. Even though it's night, I can make out the buildings, the campus, the school grounds. Then I pull up to a stoplight. I wait for the light to change so I can move on.

Suddenly, I'm bathed in red light.

The flashing red light from a police car.

I shield my eyes from the pounding, flashing light.

I hear boots crunching on pavement.

I peer through the red light and see a police officer.

He pauses and then he says, "I have to take you in."

"For what?"

"You know why."

"Speeding?"

"I have to take you in," he repeats.

"This is some bull*shit*."

I think that. I don't say that aloud.

I say, "All right, Officer."

I am at the police station, standing in front of a desk.

"Don't I get a phone call?" I say to the police officer.

"Yes," he says.

He hands me a quarter.

I look at the coin, turn it over, stare at it. I find a pay phone, drop in the quarter, listen to it clank, hear the hum of the dial tone, and dial Dell.

He picks up after a few rings.

"Hello?"

"Dell, I'm in trouble. I—"

"Hello?"

"It's me. I need you to—"

"What? Hello? What? What?"

"Dell! I got pulled over by the cops. For speeding. I'm at the po-lice station in—"

He laughs. "Oh, yeah? I'm not surprised. At all."

"Dell, I need you to come get me."

"What?" Dell's voice becomes muffled. I can hear that he's

talking to someone else. He laughs at something the other person says. He's not listening to me. He doesn't hear me. He's not *listening*.

"Dell," I say again, this time soft, wounded. "You're not listening."

I feel the anxiety rise.

"Focus, Dell," I say, quietly, and then my anxiety dissolving into defeat, I say, "Help me."

"What?" he says.

He sounds distracted, distant.

I lower my head, study the floor, and then I feel—

A light.

A white light.

Yes, I don't just see it—I *feel* this light.

The white light engulfs me.

Blinds me.

The light shocks me, nearly knocks me off my feet.

For a moment, the light frightens me.

But then the light feels warm, covers me like a huge soft white blanket.

I want to be inside this light.

I hear a quiet voice. At first, I can't make out what the voice is saying. I lean into the light so I can hear this small voice and I make out, "Daughter, you're free."

I know the voice then.

It is the voice of God.

The phone falls out of my hand.

I stare at it, hanging by its cord.

I look at it for a long time, dangling, swaying slowly, like a pendulum.

I think I hear Dell's voice laughing, talking. I'm not sure, but I can tell he's not talking to me. I grab the phone, hold it for a second, and I think, *I don't need you now*, and I hang up the phone.

I turn around and the light has gone.

I'm standing alone, in a space in the police station. The place is empty. I feel stranded. I look frantically for the police officer. I start to panic.

Where are you? Where did you go? Where is that man? Where are you? Don't go. Don't leave me here. Don't leave me!

I look at myself.

I am no longer wearing the black robe or my bikini.

I am dressed in white.

I wear a beautiful white robe, draped all around me, billowing in a warm breeze I can feel. I stare at the robe. It flows, gently. I'm mesmerized by it.

Then I'm standing in the police station in daylight—I'm bathed in daylight.

I'm alone for a moment and then the police officer appears. He smiles.

"You're free to go," he says.

"What?"

"You're free to go."

"I'm sorry, I don't understand—"

"Your bail has been paid."

"Who paid it?"

"You're free," the police officer says.

And then I wake up.

My days either take forever or blow by in a blip. I walk through each hour feeling unsettled. Agitated. Jittery. Sometimes I go eerily quiet.

I can't seem to get a grip on anything, especially my emotions. My pulse pounds. My thoughts seem to whirl inside my head at breakneck speed. And then at times my feet feel as if they are encased in cement. I'm stuck. Unable to lift myself up, unable to move an inch.

Meanwhile, around me, the kids have landed—smack, bam—right into the middle of their childhood. Stephen is ten, Seth, eight, Sydel, four. Each day blurs, all our lives accelerated, whirring by at warp speed. I like to go fast but I need to control my speed. Now my life seems to be careening out of control.

Dell is gone. Traveling with the team. He seems to be on the road more than he's at home. When he is home, we seem to pass each other without seeing each other. Missing each other. We don't appear to occupy the same space at the same time. I don't feel estranged. I feel distant. Disconnected. Alone. Even when he's here.

The school has grown so rapidly in size, enrollment, and demand that I can't control that, either. It has taken on a life of its own. A living, breathing being. I face challenges from teachers, from parents, and from myself to define what I want the school to be. I steer myself toward faith. I look for answers at my church. I don't find any yet, even though I attend services regularly. In my heart, I want to change my Montessori school to one with a Christian emphasis. That becomes clearer and clearer to me. Not everyone agrees. At one point, someone at the school asks me, "How Christian do you want it to be?" A rhetorical question. She's testing me. She knows the answer. I can hear it in her tone, her subtext: "You don't want it to be *too* Christian, do you?"

At night, unable to sleep, I wander through the house. I drift from room to room, peek in on the kids, then curl up on the living room couch. I feel empty or sometimes I feel a roiling in my gut. I close my eyes and remember my motorcycle dream. I hear the police officer's voice.

"You're free," he says.

Then why do I feel so stuck?

Over the summer, I have an opportunity to get certified in Montessori training to become a licensed Montessori educator. I want this certification because I am, in my mind, a teacher. I know that. I think everyone does. But I want the paper to prove it. However, to do so, I will have to enter an intensive program in Silver Springs, Maryland, and leave my kids for nine weeks.

I have never left my kids.

I don't leave my kids.

Then the doubt seeps in. The questions rain down on me. Is this what I want to do, what I should do? Should I take a nine-week pause in my parenting—for myself? I feel a crippling pressure to find the answers both with my personal life, with my parenting, and with Dell. The doubts persist, gnaw at me. Am I doing the right thing? Maybe I should forget about the school entirely. Maybe I should quit. Walk away. I don't know what to do. Every step I take seems tentative, uncertain. The very ground beneath my feet feels loose and shaky, as if I am tiptoeing in an earthquake.

I make the decision to go through the training even though I'll be spending more than two months away. I arrange to return on weekends. I figure out childcare. Dell. His mother. A nanny. Everyone will pitch in. I accept the help gratefully. Then I go off, alone, determined to become a certified teacher, devoted to finding my way. I leave with a conviction. I need this time for myself. To find myself. The nine weeks turtle by, but then, as if I've gone through some shimmery time lapse, I'm back home. I have earned my certification, but that's all that feels settled. I remain on edge. Dell leaves for training camp. The new NBA season and school year loom. I still can't find sleep. I pray. I ask for help. I know that I am on a search. I just don't know what I am searching *for*.

At night, I get into bed, exhausted, spent, and sleep won't come. I stare at the walls, the ceiling, I toss, turn, whisper to God, read, write in my journal, talk to myself, feeling as if I want to shout. I get out of bed in the middle of the night, wander through the house, going from room to room, checking on the kids, lurking, my nerves frayed, my arms wrapped around my clenched stomach.

One night, with Dell away on a road trip in DC, feeling so fatigued I ache, I get into bed early and, finally, mercifully, drift off to sleep—and I dream.

I'm walking in pitch darkness. The ground feels solid, but the night is so black I cannot see an inch in front of my face. I am blind and I have no idea where I'm going. I keep walking and then my instinct makes me stop abruptly. I start to take a step forward and my foot feels nothing but air. I look down and in a sliver of light I see that I have come to the edge of a steep, treacherous, frighteningly high cliff. I try to see where I am, but the darkness returns and closes in. Then from the abyss below, I hear a voice. I look down, then whip around and see only the darkness. I hear the voice again.

"Do you want to keep doing what you're doing?" the voice says.

I start to answer, stop, and realize suddenly, without a doubt, that the voice belongs to God.

I am hearing God's voice.

I have to go back, I think. *I have to go back where I came from.*

I felt safe there. Uncertain and confused, but safe.

I turn around. I look back, take one step, and stop. My stomach starts to churn and then it twists into a knot and begins to cramp. I feel sick.

I begin to shake. My entire body trembles. I look back down over the edge of the cliff and stare into the abyss, into the cold darkness. I can't see a thing. I see only pitch black.

"You're asking me to step off the cliff, into the *void*?"

I creak the words out. I barely speak them.

"It's so dark," I say.

"Do you trust Me?" the voice says.

I crane my neck slightly, look behind me, and I realize that what lies there is my past, my former self. My uncertainty. My doubt.

I need to leave that behind.

I need to move forward.

Into the darkness.

I need to take a step—one step, one tiny step—over the edge of the cliff.

Behind me, I hear a soft, sweet voice.

"Do you trust Me?"

I lift my foot, stop, put it back down.

"Trust Me," the voice says.

I take the step into the darkness.

Feeling my tears come, I whisper, "Save me."

12

Saved

I WAKE UP.

I don't know where I am.

I can't move. I wait—

Ten seconds. Twenty. Thirty.

Where am I?

Am I—awake?

Or . . . wait . . .

Am I still asleep?

I grip the side of the bed, peek over the edge. I expect to see darkness. The abyss. Instead, I see the floor. I sit up and look around my bedroom.

Then I feel my hands shaking.

My lips start to tremble.

I can't catch my breath.

I feel like I'm falling. Plummeting into a chasm of darkness.

Down. Down. Down.

I'm NOT awake.

I'm *falling*.

I gasp.

I look around my bedroom again. I take a deep breath and center myself. I see my journal on the nightstand. I reach for it and start to write. I scribble frantically, not sure I even recognize the words I put down. Gibberish. I stop. Look at the page. Tear it out of the journal. Stare at a new blank page.

What should I write?

I have no idea what to say.

Suddenly I know. I know what I feel. I understand what is happening.

I calculate the time. I confirm the day.

Wednesday.

I will go to church tonight.

I will go to services tonight at seven.

I close my journal with a snap that startles me.

I float through the day. I don't know how I drive to work or do my job or interact with anyone. I feel as if I'm in a trance. Then I feel pulled. Drawn to a purpose. I no longer feel afraid. I feel—numb. Somehow, the day ends, I drive home, the kids barely speaking, lost in their own worlds, and then we arrive home. At seven, I go to church alone.

I feel as if I'm semiconscious, out of my body, watching myself. In a fog, I see myself walking into our church in Charlotte, the Central Church of God. I walk to my seat. I sit, my body erect, rigid. I have been *pulled* here. Something like destiny has drawn me. I feel that. And I know something is about to happen. I don't know what.

I don't know when. I inch forward in my seat, my nerves firing, popping, my body tensed, my mind calm and alert at the same time.

I glance at the people around me, a sea of faces, of bodies, numbering a thousand, two thousand, maybe even more. I feel the music of the service wash over me. The voices of the choir stir me. I watch their faces caught up in the spirit, their eyes closed, their mouths wide with song. Their voices swirl toward me, the music nearly lifting me out of my seat. They finish their hymn and the pastor begins leading prayers and I murmur the prayers along with him, at one with the congregation. Then silence descends. It feels immense. The pastor starts his sermon. He grips the podium on both sides and, his voice rumbling, speaks to all of us, but I hear something different. I look up, and edge even farther forward in my seat. I believe he is speaking directly to me. We lock eyes as he says—

"If you're tired of doing the same thing, then do something different."

He doesn't address me by name. He doesn't have to.

He is expressing what I felt in my cliff dream. He is speaking the words that bored into me as I stared into the blinding dark of the abyss. God is speaking through him. He is speaking to me. I hear Him.

I start to cry.

The pastor speaks with a force that I have never heard come from him before. His words rush over each other, each syllable burrowing into my soul.

"*If* you have a heavy heart. If you know you need to *change*. If you want to leave here a different person. If you want to bring Jesus into your heart. Allow him in. He'll take over from there. Allow. Him. *In*.

Who wants to come to the altar today? Do you want to come to the altar today? Do *you* want to give yourself to Jesus?"

For a moment, I don't recognize what's happening to me. Then I identify my movements. I tick them off, one by one. I'm standing. I'm sliding out of the pew. I'm walking toward the front of the congregation. I feel nervous and then I feel embarrassed. I know everyone here and everyone knows me. I'm so visible. I feel everyone's eyes on me. Then fear overwhelms me. My body trembles. I start to panic. But I keep moving. I laser my eyes forward and with every step, I sense the congregation following me with their eyes, tracking me. What are they thinking?

Why is she going up to the altar?

What is going on with her?

Are they all looking at me?

Tears slide down my face, but I still walk, and then, suddenly, I have a change of mind, of heart, and I think, *I don't care.* I don't care what anyone thinks. I am going through with this. I have been invited to do this. I am going by invitation only. I am going to do this.

God will show me the way. No. God will show me a *new* way.

I know this as surely as I know my own name—

Faith is an action. Faith is about doing. Faith is about taking this walk.

I peek up at heaven—I squint toward heaven—and through my tears, I say, "Lord, I am ready to follow You, for real. Forever. I trust You."

The fear flitters away. Instead, I feel a surge of strength. My soul feels pumped up. Now, with each step I take, I feel more solid, more certain, more determined. And I feel powerful.

My first faith walk, I think.

Then, somehow, I know.

A truth arrives. Inserts itself.

I feel myself change.

It almost feels as if my insides have become scrambled. My heart jostled. My soul rearranged.

"God," I say, "I'm going to trust that if I allow You to work on me, to allow You to work inside me and change me—my life will change. All my doubts, fears, uncertainties will vanish. Because I know You only want the good for us. That's all You want. So I give myself to You."

Then I feel it.

The spirit.

The spirit has entered me.

Time freezes.

Then I see myself—

Kneeling in front of the pastor.

He reaches out and touches my head.

An electric shock fires through me. My own personal lightning.

Then—trembling.

My entire body shaking. Shivering.

Other hands reaching toward me. Touching me.

My entire self, my being . . . warming, burning . . . an unbearable weight crushes me—and then a beautiful white light appears and pours through me.

Soothing me. Cloaking me.

I am swaddled in light.

I try to look up but all I can see is this light because I am sobbing.

And then—remarkably—I am lifted up.

I rise.

Whatever else I have felt before has been replaced by a thrill. A jolt of excitement.

I feel new. I feel powerful. I feel clarity. I feel goodness.

I am saved.

13

The Gatekeeper

THE NEXT morning, I wake up with a thirst. My soul feels parched.

I lie in bed for a few seconds, immobilized, paralyzed in the state between awake and asleep, my body feeling unattached to me, far away, not my own. My mind grapples with consciousness, searching for clarity, trying to get a grip on this brand-new day.

That's how this day feels.

New.

I am in you now.

I feel that.

I want that.

I am a new arrival, I think.

Then, I think—Wednesdays.

I will begin my *new* with Wednesdays.

I will make Wednesdays my Sabbath.

Sunday, the usual Sabbath, I will implement as a rest day, a day for prayer and for family time. We will go to church together Sundays, then stick together the rest of the day as much as we can, sharing our time, ourselves, just—being.

And from now on, I will make Wednesday my day of fasting and prayer. Except for sips of water, I will take no food from sunup until sundown. I will give myself this day as a time of reflection and prayer. A midweek respite.

I also embrace Romans 12:2: "Don't copy the behavior and customs of this world, but let God transform you into a new person by changing the way you think. Then you will know God's will for you, which is good and pleasing and perfect."

Transform myself.

I make a decision.

I will cleanse.

I will give up drinking and embrace the study of Scripture.

I will work on myself. I will fix myself. I will change myself.

Control what is in your control.

That's all you can do.

So that's what I will do—with all my heart, with all my might, with all my soul.

I swing my legs off the bed.

I look at the Bible on my nightstand. I pick it up and thumb through the pages, stopping at the Scripture I'd read before falling asleep the night before.

"And we know that all things work together for good to those who love God, to those who are called to His purpose."

God's Word, I think.

I close my eyes and visualize what that means.

All things work together for the good.

It's about having faith and not having fear. Trusting in God's plan. And acting with as much goodness and patience as we can, knowing that it will eventually work out for the good. In the meantime, we have to negotiate through human weaknesses, faults, and sin, and find goodness where we can. When it comes to parenting, I know this much. You cannot parent out of fear. You have to parent out of purpose, into faith, and embrace every morsel of goodness.

I vow to do that—to find goodness, asking for God's help along the way. I have always had belief. I will now have active faith. I close the Bible, stretch, and feel myself getting out of bed, every nerve ending hot-wired.

When the kids and I gather downstairs for devotion, I'm practically bursting with renewed energy. The kids don't notice. The energy exists inside me, in my spirit. I may mention something about a renewal of prayer, a renewal of spirit, of being saved, of walking with God. I don't recall. If I do, I doubt that anyone responds. Maybe Stephen nods, or Seth yawns, or Sydel squirms. I want to say, *I'm feeling a profound difference. A difference within me,* but I don't say anything. In time, they may see the change. For now, I just know that I have so much to read, to learn, to *do.*

For one thing, I know how Christian I want my school to be.

Driving into school, that staffer's question strikes me like a slap. It would be as if I'd asked in return, "How Montessori do you want this *Montessori* school to be?"

It seems clear to me.

Either you're Montessori or you're not.

Either you're Christian or you're not.

You can't be sort of either one.

In all the way or out.

I don't do anything that day. I take my time gathering myself. I try to be patient, understanding, kind. I feel that I am this way naturally, but I'm now more conscious, more active. Time goes on. I find myself turning to God not only daily, but constantly, as if I am having a continuous conversation with a close and caring friend. I take time to pray, to read Scripture. I jot down my favorite verses and post them all over the house. I pray for my family and I pray for help at school. I ask God for guidance. I don't push. I embrace patience. I know that God acts in His own time. I remember the story of Sarah in the Bible. God promised the supposedly barren Sarah that she would get pregnant. She laughed because she didn't believe Him. Plus, she was ninety years old. But she did get pregnant with Isaac and nursed him herself. A miracle. Miracles happen, but they take patience, perseverance, and prayer.

I start to have dreams about the school. Nightmares. In one, two members of my staff who have expressed doubt about our mission appear at the school's front doors, which are locked. They bang on the doors with their fists, trying to force their way inside. I stand on the other side, pushing against the doors, trying to hold them off. Behind them, I see someone else at my school, a member of school leadership, my most vocal opponent, urging them on. In real life, I have butted heads with him repeatedly. I have held my ground, have not backed down. Lately, I have prayed for help, asking God how to approach him. I have tried kindness, goodness, patience even as I felt attacked. I'm not sure what to do, what action to take. I awake, sweating, my heart racing.

A few nights later, I fall into a deep sleep. A crack of thunder jars me awake. I sit up in bed.

I know instinctively that God has something to tell me. I feel that in my gut. I know that from our conversations, my prayers. I am instantly alert, ready to take in His message.

"Okay, I'm listening," I say, looking skyward, almost laughing. Then I feel nervous, unsettled. I *know* God has something to tell me.

I get out of bed. I'm on the move, acting purely on instinct. I'm not thinking. I'm *doing*. I check the clock at my bedside: 3:30 a.m. I feel myself walking out of my bedroom and into the front foyer. The pat-pat-pat of rain pelts our roof and walls like drumbeats. I flinch at each beat. The rain doesn't let up. It remains loud, insistent. I walk to the front door. I know I have to open the door in the middle of this rainstorm. I have no idea why. It seems crazy, but I know I have to do this.

I open the front door and look outside. The rain pours down in sheets, wet line drives whipping down from the sky. Our driveway—a semicircle—has flooded. I stare into the night, looking at a small stream instead of our solid driveway. All I see is water. It seems surreal. It seems—biblical.

Then my eyes pick up something swimming in the center of the stream.

A snake.

A blacksnake slicing through the water.

My mouth opens, slams shut.

Stunned, I say the obvious aloud. "It's a snake."

I don't feel frightened.

I feel *told*. Informed. I feel unsteady in the doorway.

I know that God has given me a message. I know what He is saying.

The snake symbolizes the person who has been stirring up

dissension at the school. The man with whom I have been butting heads.

I know what I have to do.

I murmur a quiet "Thank you."

I shut the front door and go back to my bedroom.

The next morning at school, I make a flurry of phone calls. For the good of the school and for the good of my state of mind, I make the change I have to make. By the end of the day, I have told that member of school leadership to step down.

More time passes. I continue to work on myself. I read the Bible, jot down more verses that speak to me, and again post them all over the house on sticky notes. Sundays, during our family meeting, I write a new verse on the whiteboard in the kitchen. I read it aloud, sometimes ask the kids to read it, too. During the week, I keep the Scripture with me in my journal or on an index card, referring to it frequently.

On Wednesdays, I fast, but I feed on the Word. I read the Bible before I go to sleep and first thing when I wake up. I write constantly—on Post-its, in the margins of books, but mostly in journals. I scribble down my dreams, thoughts, prayers. I go through journal after journal.

I read this from Matthew 6:6—

"When you pray, go into your room, close the door and pray to your Father, who is unseen. Then your Father, who sees what is done in secret, will reward you."

I pray in the living room, in the kitchen, in bed, and even in the car. But from my readings—especially that verse from Matthew—and talking to other church members, I know that I need my own private space to pray. Someplace isolated. No distractions. A quiet, undisclosed spot where I can disappear and be alone with God.

A prayer closet.

I choose, literally, my closet.

I search the house for another quiet spot, maybe a small room where no one will disturb me. But I can't find any other space or room that feels right.

So I decide to turn my bedroom closet into a prayer closet.

I shut myself inside the closet. I bring my bibles, my journals, and the prayers and Scriptures that I've written down on Post-its. I bring a tiny candle. I have a walk-in closet so I have plenty of room to spread out. I intend to get into my prayer closet every day, but I cut myself some slack, knowing that I probably won't be able to make that happen.

When I get into the closet, I light a candle, turn off the light, spread out, make myself comfortable. For a minimum of thirty minutes, I try to lose myself in quiet. I search for a kind of fellowship with God. I begin a conversation with Him and then I just—reflect. Meditate. I find the prayer closet serene, peaceful, soothing. I dissolve inside. I can feel my being float away. Sometimes, my mind wanders. I won't be able to meditate or pray or even talk with God and I'll start thinking about an issue at school or with a family member or even something mundane, like what I want to cook for dinner. And sometimes, I fall asleep. When I wake up, I feel guilty. And I praise God that I didn't burn the house down.

"I'm sorry, Lord," I say. "I got in here, shut the door, turned off the lights, and my mind started wandering. The next thing I knew I was asleep—"

I cut myself off. I realize that most of the time, we pray when things are not going well in our lives or we want something specific from God. We seek help or we have an ask. I believe, from all my readings and from my instinct, that all God wants is fellowship. Commitment. Connection. I start to feel that the effort of getting into the closet and sitting there—even if my mind wanders, even if I fall asleep—is enough.

God doesn't want anything, I think. He just wants us to be with Him.

Sometimes at night, the Word wakes me. A three a.m. to four a.m. spiritual alarm clock.

At least, I think that's what wakes me.

I'm not sure. But something—a gut feeling— stirs inside me and jolts me awake. It feels like an electric shock pulsing through me.

When it happens, I blink through the fog of sleep, open my eyes, and within seconds, I know that I have to get out of bed and walk.

Prayer walk.

I need to see my kids.

I want to pray over them.

I have always prayed for them. I pray for them daily. I listen for them. I fast weekly, on Wednesdays, to flush out the poisons, to dispose of my physical and mental toxins. I clearly see my role. I am the caretaker of our home. I feel responsible for keeping our home peaceful and safe. I need to be present and aware. I vow not to be intrusive. Instead, I intend to be a participant, an observer, the night watchman. The gatekeeper.

I gather Scriptures I've written on scraps of paper and index cards, stuff them into the pockets of my robe, check the clock—3:00 a.m.—sigh, wonder, ask myself why I always do these things at three o'clock in the morning, shake my head, and feeling a sense of necessity and responsibility, walk purposely into each kid's room, one at a time. I enter the room as quietly as I can. I pause in the doorway, allow my eyes to adjust to the darkness, scan the room with an inner searchlight. Then I step farther in, look at my child sleeping, and my eyes fill up. I walk to the bottom of the bed, reach out my hand, and touch my child's foot. I whisper a prayer. Some nights, I get on my knees and pray. Some nights I sit on the floor and watch my child sleep. Some nights, I pull over a chair, sit down, lower my head, and pray.

One night, as I watch Seth sleep, he wakes up.

"Mom! What are you doing?"

"I'm sorry, honey. It's nothing. I'm just checking on you. That's all."

"You scared me."

"I'm so sorry. I didn't mean to. Go back to sleep."

He mumbles something and shuts his eyes.

The next night, I prayer walk into Seth's room again. I touch his feet. I touch his head. I sit at the foot of his bed and watch him sleep. He wakes up again.

"*Mom!*"

"I know. I'm sorry."

"What are you *doing?*"

"I'm just checking on you."

He mumbles something and pulls the covers over his head.

The third time I prayer walk into his room, I touch his feet, his head, and sit quietly. He wakes up and looks at me.

I smile.

He mumbles.

I leave.

What Seth—and Stephen and Sydel—don't realize is that not only do I watch them sleep, touch their feet, their heads, and pray over them, but I also jot down lines of Scripture on scraps of paper and stuff them under their mattresses. One day, when we flip the mattresses, they find the Scriptures.

"What are all these random pieces of paper?" Stephen says.

"Oh, those?" I say. "They're Scriptures."

Stephen looks at me. By now, all the kids have gotten used to me prayer walking through the house and watching them sleep.

"You put them there while I was asleep?"

"Yeah."

"Seth and Sydel, too?"

"Sure."

I believe that I can read inside his head. I know that he's thinking—

Why do you do that? Never mind.

"Good thoughts, prayers might seep into you while you sleep," I say. "Keep you safe."

Stephen shakes his head.

I want to say, "I'm the gatekeeper," but I just smile.

I have become saved. I have committed to my walk with God. I have changed my life. I've given up alcohol. I pray. I actively work toward seeing the good in every situation. I try not to act irrationally when it comes to big decisions without careful thought and prayer. I see each day as part of a spiritual process. I look at every twenty-four hours as a piece of a whole, a chapter in the holy book of life. I end each day, after my kids have gone to bed, with a final reflection, a survey of the previous twenty-four hours.

Assessing the day. Reviewing the day, the highlights, the not-so-wonderful moments. Then—praying. Getting into bed. Turning out the lights. Allowing myself—my entire being—to become swallowed into darkness. Looking back at the day one last time, I say, in prayer, "I tried today. There was no fake hustle. It was real. Genuine all day. I gave it everything I had."

That's all I—or anyone—can do.

I believe that's all God asks.

14

God's Time

SOMETIMES I wonder if I got saved just in time to face the challenges of parenthood. I know that right before I got saved, I felt I was flailing, searching for a direction. I prayed and God answered me in my dreams. He led me to that Wednesday night in church when I got saved. More than that, He saved me.

To this day, more than twenty years later, that night—being saved—still impacts me so deeply, so profoundly. I continue to marvel at the revelations I feel, realizations I've come to. So many of us pray to God out of desperation. We turn to God when we feel we've come to the end of the line. We feel that we're out of options. We pray as a last resort. We throw our own personal Hail Mary pass. We need help *now*. We have this problem *now*. We need the answer *now*. Strangely—more often than not—it seems that God takes His sweet time. It's so hard to be patient when we're in the middle of a crisis or we feel urgency. But we can't rush God. And if nothing else, I've learned that He will provide answers at exactly the right time. God's time. Even if it doesn't feel like the right time to us.

God's time.

After I get saved, and then baptized, I surrender and dive head-first into remodeling my entire life—no alcohol, fasting, praying, attending church regularly, studying Scripture. I feel my transformation starting to occur. And while I've embraced my walk with God, it feels as if all the challenges of parenting suddenly come rushing at me. I have to up my parenting game. As they grow older, Stephen and Seth offer new hurdles for me. Two boys. Brothers. Close friends. Fierce foes, especially on the basketball court. Both smart, talented, headstrong.

I do believe there is something real about birth order. When I look at Stephen, I recognize myself. Always trying to please. The peacemaker. Full of fun. Engaging. Emotional. Usually taking on his challenges with joy and enthusiasm. A typical first child. At first, Seth is silly, goofy, looking for fun. But then he becomes a typical second child. More mysterious. Quieter. He withdraws. He doesn't communicate as openly or as frequently. He keeps his emotions close to his chest. Strong, silent. Guarded. Very careful about letting you in, revealing himself.

All younger siblings—especially those of the same sex—experience some sibling rivalry and often middle children get squeezed between the older sibling and younger sibling. As I've learned, sometimes the toughest place to be is stuck in the middle. While Stephen engages, communicates, Seth mumbles or swallows his words, or says nothing. He may express himself with a grunt, silence, a roll of the eyes. But whenever Seth and I talk substantively, he reveals who he is—whip smart, independent, opinionated, his own person.

On the court, I see the evolution of Stephen and Seth's relationship. As the younger brother, Seth looks up to Stephen and tries to emulate him. As he grows and the boys play on the same team, Seth tries to outdo Stephen. He wants to stand out on his own, to emerge from Stephen's substantial shadow. Seth longs to create his own space, to throw his own shadow for others to stand in. The two boys play against each other often in practice. They treat each other as rivals. They go *at* each other. Once—and perhaps more than once—Seth, believing that the coaches have given Stephen preferential treatment, gets into it with Stephen. Pushing. Shoving. Slapping. And then—full-out fighting. Rolling on the floor, whaling on each other. Dell, serving as assistant coach, dives in and pulls them apart.

"It's natural," Dell says to me later, shrugging, dismissing their fight. "Brothers going at it."

I agree. It is natural. But it's also upsetting.

Seth operates at his own pace, moving to the sound of his own beat, the rhythm he hears in his head. To most people, he may seem quiet, shy, even distant, but I'm his mother and I can feel that rhythm and see his mind working at warp speed. While Stephen goes out of his way to comply, to get along, to seek my acceptance, Seth often goes the other way, showing defiance, looking to test me. Frankly, this frustrates me, but as Seth finds out time and time again, I don't back down. Defying me does not work. Still, I told myself early on that when it comes to breaking our house rules or disobeying me, I won't sweat the small stuff—too much. I will parent by the "three strikes and you're out rule." Unfortunately, I'm an impatient umpire. I rarely get to three strikes.

"That's one strike," I say to Seth when he talks back. Shortly after, he goes there again.

"That's it," I say. "Go to your room."

He looks at me in disbelief. "I thought we get three strikes."

"Nope. Two strikes. Sorry, dude. I used the parents' prerogative to change my mind."

Head down, murmuring something I can't hear—probably something I wouldn't want to hear—Seth, showing his usual swag, slowly walks upstairs. He mumbles something and makes a sound I will come to identify with him.

"Tzuh," he mutters.

15

I Can Do All Things

I can do all things through Christ who strengthens me.

—Philippians 4:13

TWELVE-YEAR-OLD STEPHEN sits at the end of our oversized kitchen table. He slumps over a mound of books, notebooks, pens, a laptop. This table, as long as one you would find in a conference room, comfortably seats sixteen people. Right now, Stephen seems dwarfed by its enormity and overwhelmed by the task in front of him—completing his first week's homework as a seventh grader at his new school, Charlotte Christian.

Until this year, Stephen has attended the Montessori school I started. He has never faced this amount of homework. He has learned how to study and how to sift through information. He's learned how to take a practical approach to tasks he faces, and he's learned time management. But this task feels insurmountable.

I have left Stephen alone to navigate his boatload of homework, but I have made several cameo appearances in the kitchen—making a cup of tea, grabbing a snack, scribbling a note on the whiteboard on the wall, all flimsy excuses to check on my son's progress and well-being. Even from the other room—even from upstairs—I can sense his distress and frustration. He doesn't have to say anything. I can just feel it. I am his mother and mothers know these things. We have an unspoken connection. He doesn't have to utter a word. He would never complain—that's not his way. But I know what he's feeling. Again, sometimes I believe I can see inside my son's head.

The third or fourth time I drift into the kitchen, I move toward the counter. As I reach for a cup in the cabinet, I glance at him at the far end of the table. He looks so small and far away. He drops his shoulders even farther and I see tears forming in his eyes. He looks up at me.

"Mom."

I move toward him and take a seat next to him.

"What is it, son?"

"I—"

He sniffs, fights back his tears. He bites his lip. He refuses to cry.

"I can't do this."

"What do you mean?"

I speak quietly, not in judgment nor in criticism. I ask him a simple, legitimate question, to explain, to get him to think.

"What can't you do?"

He shrugs at the pile of books in front of him. "I have to get this all done by tomorrow. It's too much."

"Well," I say.

He waves both arms in frustration. "Look at all this."

"Okay." I gently lay my hand on his forearm. "Now, tell me, what have you learned in Montessori about time management? Where did you go wrong here?"

Stephen frowns, looks past me as if he's searching for the answer.

"I didn't plan it out," he says.

"What else?"

"I waited until the last minute."

"And what have you learned about facing a large task? How do you approach that task?"

He taps his fingers on the table. "You break it down into parts."

"So," I say, "you have a couple hours before you have to get up to bed. Use your skills. Break this down into parts. Do what you can. And tomorrow, what are you going to do?"

"Tell my teacher that I couldn't get it all done."

"Right."

"Take the consequences," he says.

"Stephen," I say, lightly gripping his arm, "you cannot be afraid. You have the skills to succeed here. You have it in you. This isn't about homework. It's about managing your life. You got to dig deep, apply everything you've learned, and move forward, little by little. You can do it."

He looks at me then with the strength and resolve that I identify as unique to him. His character. These qualities define him. These qualities will take him far.

"You can't let fear paralyze you," I say.

"I never will," he says.

I stand, rub his shoulders for a second or two, start to leave, and turn back to look at him. Stephen opens a book and begins jotting notes in his notebook.

He's a fighter, I think. *He may look slight and unthreatening, but you don't see his spirit, his soul. This boy—this young man—is a fierce warrior.*

Two years later.

Stephen has started freshman year at Charlotte Christian. One afternoon, through the back window, Dell and I watch Stephen shoot. Shot after shot. *Swish. Swish. Swish.* He sprints after every occasional miss, scoops up the ball, turns and fires a putback. He's tireless, never stops moving. To rest, he shoots free throws. We watch him from here, his too-big jersey flapping over his skinny shoulders, and he looks even smaller than his five-feet, six-inch, one-hundred-thirty-pound frame. He looks scrawny. He's fourteen, but to me, his mother, he looks about eight. He dribbles once, twice, exhales, flicks in another free throw from his hip. *Swish.*

"He has a good eye," I say.

"Yeah," Dell says. "And a poor release point."

I scowl at him. I'm about to defend our son, but then I realize that Dell is not criticizing him. He's thinking about how to help him.

"What do you mean?" I say.

"He's so small," Dell says. "If he shoots from down here, at his hip, or even his chest, he'll never get his shot off. Taller guys will block it."

"Pretty much everyone is taller."

"Pretty much."

"Maybe he'll grow," I say.

"Maybe," Dell says.

Later, I see Dell working with Stephen. Dell, one of the NBA's best shooters, demonstrates a new release point. He gently moves Stephen's hands higher. He shows Stephen how to cradle the ball, shoot it quickly from right above his forehead. He's not merely correcting Stephen's shot. He's completely changing it. Overhauling it. Remaking it. If he were an architect working on a house, he would be tearing up the previous blueprint and starting all over. Stephen watches his father, hands on his hips, nodding, taking in everything that Dell says. Then Dell hands him the basketball. Stephen starts to shoot from the free-throw line. Dell moves him closer to the basket, only slightly farther from the hoop than a layup. Stephen holds the ball the way Dell showed him. He looks at Dell for approval. Dell nods. Steph holds the ball higher, his release point close to the top of his head. Dell nods again. Steph looks at the hoop and shoots.

He misses.

The ball clanks off the back of the rim.

Even from here, I can hear Stephen shout in frustration. He looks awkward. Uncomfortable. Unsure.

Breaking him down, I think. *Then building him up.*

I know that's Dell's plan. And I know Dell's right.

Dell says something to Stephen, claps his hands, pats him on the back, and comes inside.

We watch through the window, silently, side by side, as Stephen takes another shot from close in, nearly a layup. He misses. He shakes his head, retrieves the ball, slaps it with both hands.

"He has to change his shot," Dell says, quietly, with certainty.

"Are you sure?"

Dell looks at me. "There are two or three things I know for sure. One is how to shoot a basketball."

Dell has given Stephen instruction. I give my son a plan.

"I have to shoot the basketball quicker," he tells me.

"Quicker release," I say.

"Yes. And Dad says I have to release it higher."

We're at the kitchen table, sharing a snack.

"Show me," I say.

Stephen demonstrates, putting both hands above his head, pantomiming his new shot, curling and flicking his wrists.

"You open to this?" I ask.

"Yeah. I'm just not comfortable."

"Yet," I say.

Stephen shrugs.

"It sounds like good advice," I say.

"I guess."

I pat Stephen's arm. "Your father is not just some guy who plays pickup ball Saturday mornings at the Y. He's Dell Curry."

Stephen smiles. "Yeah. He can shoot."

"So what's your plan?"

"Let's go outside," Stephen says.

We go outside to the basketball court. We set up spots, starting with layups from either side. Then we set up a spot two steps back from that, on either side. We continue moving farther away from the hoop at two-step intervals until we've gone beyond the three-point line.

"How do you think this should work?" I ask him.

Stephen thinks for a second and says, "I need to earn the right to move back to the next spot."

"Okay. How do you do that?"

"I have to make ninety percent of my shots. Then I can move."

"Wow. You're tough."

"Eighteen of twenty shots, then I'll go to the next spot."

I hand him the ball. "Have at it."

I stand aside, watching as Stephen rapidly fires in layup after layup. He makes most, but still looks uncomfortable. He shakes his head.

"Only made fifteen," he says, whistling out a breath. He glances longingly at the next spot, a few feet away. He shakes his head.

"Twenty more," he says.

"Have fun," I say, heading into the house.

Stephen shoots for hours. I stay inside, keeping a silent watch through the window. As the shadows lengthen, I see that he's only made it two spots back from his initial layup spot. Then, I move away from the window and start thinking about dinner. I hear a scream. I rush to the window, praying he hasn't hurt himself. I look out and see Stephen, red-faced, walking in a circle. He then prowls the baseline of our backyard basketball court. He looks miserable. I decide to stay inside. He needs to work this out for himself. He shoots until I call him inside. He doesn't say much during dinner

Stephen practices his shooting every day—day after day—for hours. I watch him periodically through the window. I don't like what I see. He seems increasingly frustrated. One day, used to see ing flashes of movement—Stephen running after errant shots, pulling up to shoot his jump shot—I realize that I haven't noticed him at all. I stand up on my tiptoes and see Stephen—sitting on the ball at the free-throw line. He holds his head in his hands. I wipe my hands on a dish towel and walk outside, as casually as I can.

"Hey," I say. "What's going on?"

Stephen looks up at me. I can see that he has been crying.

"I can't do this," he says.

I want to bite my lip, but all I do is nod sympathetically. Stephen swipes at his cheek. "I'm not going to do this anymore."

"Okay," I say. "That's your decision. Your choice."

He sniffs, nods.

"You don't have to play basketball. There's no law, no decree, and, honestly, no pressure."

Stephen says nothing.

"If you decide to give it up, that's fine. It's your choice. Completely your call. But I don't see a halfway. You want to give it up, then give it up. Give up this whole basketball idea. The whole thing. It's obviously not worth it."

He lifts his head and squints past me.

"But I want you to realize that your dad has shared with you what you need to do if you want to get to where you want to be. You have ideas, I know. Plans. Aspirations. Dreams. You want to do well in high school. Go to a major college. I know you've talked about going to Duke. I know that's on your mind."

I pause to check his reaction. Uncomfortable sitting on the ball, he stands up, paces on the foul line, allowing the ball to roll toward me. I pick it up and cradle it against my side.

"He changed everything," Stephen says. "I've had to remake my whole shot."

"I know," I say. "Dad was telling you what you had to do. But now it's up to you if you want to implement that, keep working toward your goals, and getting better, getting your shot *right*."

Stephen stops pacing and sniffs again.

"Or," I say.

I wait.

"Or?" he says, looking at me.

"Or do you want to *quit*?"

For a long time, Stephen says nothing. He seems to stare into the backboard, studying it, perhaps trying to see a glimpse of his future. Finally, he turns to me, offering a thin smile. I know he's made a decision. He nods at the ball. I don't move. I hold the ball tighter against my hip.

"Are you sure?" I say.

He nods.

I hand him the ball. He seems relieved and then determined. He dribbles the ball once, twice, and sets up behind the free-throw line. He bends his knees, and—his hands placed above his head, exactly as Dell taught him—he shoots.

Swish.

He never looks back.

By the middle of his sophomore year, Stephen has become Charlotte Christian's starting point guard and leading scorer. Locally and soon statewide, he develops a reputation as an exceptional—maybe even unique—shooter. Coaches and fans comment that they have never seen anyone shoot with such accuracy from such long distance, and with such a quick release, making his shot nearly impossible to block. The team itself has realized unprecedented success, heading toward what will be the first of three consecutive conference titles and three straight state playoff appearances. But even with all this success and potential, I don't hesitate to call Shonn Brown, Stephen's coach, with bad news.

"Hi, Coach," I say on the phone. "Unfortunately, Stephen won't be attending practice today."

"Why? Is he sick?"

"No. He didn't do the dishes."

Coach Brown pauses so long that I worry he has either hung up or passed out.

"Are you there?" I ask.

"Yes. I think we have a bad connection. It sounded like you said Stephen's missing practice because *he didn't do the dishes.*"

"That's what I said."

"Are you kidding?"

"I am not kidding."

"We're talking about missing practice because of *dishes*, am I right? I can't—"

Coach Brown doesn't finish his sentence. I can almost hear him gathering his thoughts, formulating his argument, trying to figure out how to come to Stephen's defense. I sense him desperately wanting to turn this decision around. I want to explain that he can't turn it around.

"I know that family is important to you," he says, his voice hesitant and slightly muffled.

"That's not true," I say. "Family is not important to me. Family is primary. Family is crucial. Family is everything. *Important* doesn't come close to describing it."

"No, I know, I get that. I do. But in Stephen's defense, everybody hates doing the dishes."

"Why is that?" I ask. "It's not that hard. You don't have to wash the dishes by hand. In our house, you load and unload the dishwasher. It's not a big deal."

"You may think that," he says. "But for a lot of guys, it's a big problem. According to my wife, I never do it right. The glasses go upstairs. The dishes go downstairs. I don't know why. I don't see that it matters. It doesn't matter how I load the dishwasher, she rearranges everything anyway."

"What are you saying?"

"I don't know. Look. Here's the problem. If Stephen misses practice, he can't start. That's the rule."

"Exactly," I say. "That's your rule. You have a team rule. We have a family rule. If you don't do your chores, you don't go to practice. I warned him. More than once. I reminded him several times during the week, 'Steph, you know you've got dishes, right?' He just tuned me out. 'I know, Mom, yeah, yeah, yeah, I know.' I said, 'It's just a reminder. You need to get in the kitchen and do the dishes.' He said, 'Oh, I will.' Well, guess what? He didn't."

"What if you called this strike one, or even strike two? You could give him another chance. You know, three strikes and you're out?"

"In our house, you only get two strikes. If you're lucky."

"What about—I'm brainstorming here, trying to think of a compromise—isn't there something he can do to make it up?"

"Make it up? Like what?"

"I don't know. Do twice as many dishes next week?"

"Seriously?"

Another pause, and then Coach Brown says in a voice tinged with panic, "We need him to start. We've got a big game coming up."

"You know what I say to that?"

"I think I do."

"Last night, the kids came in for dinner. They were hungry. They asked what's for dinner. I said, 'Nothing. There is no dinner. I don't have any dinner. You know why? I don't have any plates to put any food on because *Stephen didn't do the dishes.*'"

The phone goes silent.

"Shonn," I say. "Are you there?"

"I'm here. I can't start him. I really can't."

"Stephen should have thought about that before. In our home, family comes first. Family is more important than any practice or any game."

"I hear that. Loud and clear. You're going to stick to your rules and I'm going to stick to mine. No favoritism."

"In the long run, Stephen will be better for it."

"I believe that. In the short run, he is going to hear about it from me, too."

Coach Brown, a man of honor and a man of his word, sticks to his rule. Stephen misses practice and doesn't start the next game.

I hate disappointing my kids. I can't abide seeing them hurt or angry even when I know I have made the right decision. I reminded Stephen so many times to do the dishes that I realized he was starting to rely on me to manage him. That's not going to work. I have to train my kids to manage themselves. That's what this is about. Yes, everyone has to do their part to keep the Big Machine running. At the same time, they have to learn to be their own managers.

When I tell Stephen that he has to miss practice, he doesn't argue or push back. He accepts his consequences. He has no other choice. He knows he can't change my mind. If nothing else, my kids have come to accept this one truth about me.

I may not always be right, but I'm always sure.

16

We Don't Date, We Mate

WHEN IT comes to dating, I have a hard-and fast rule.

Don't.

Or as I say to my kids, "We don't date, we mate."

I realize that may be harsh and possibly a bit extreme.

So I compromise.

No dating until you turn sixteen.

That seems fair to me. More than fair.

I explain this repeatedly to Stephen who's nearly sixteen and *very* interested in girls and Seth who's thirteen and starting to show an interest as well. I allow the boys to travel in a coed pack, boys and girls together, a group of friends going to a party or a game, as long as they stay in their group, don't pair off, and come in before curfew— ten o'clock sophomore year, eleven o'clock junior year, midnight for seniors.

I call that more than fair.

As girls start hovering around Stephen, I remember my senior year of high school. I shudder when I think about Rick, the older guy I got involved with and how badly that turned out. I want to protect my kids from experiencing anything like that. I begin worrying about Sydel even now as a nine-year-old fourth grader.

I know that I have acquired a reputation for being the "strict mom." I can sense that whenever I attend one of the kids' games. I ask Stephen about it.

"Why are people so scared of me?"

He laughs. Nervously.

"You know."

"No, I don't. Tell me."

"Well, it's because you're a little stricter than most of the other moms."

"A little stricter?"

"Yeah. When it comes to dating and stuff."

"Interesting," I say. "Tell me about that."

"Oh, wow, look at the time. I have a big algebra test tomorrow. I better study."

"We're not finished with this conversation," I say as Stephen flies up the stairs to his room.

Over the next few days, I learn from him and from chatter around the school that Stephen is the kid who when asked by his friends to explain his restrictions, curfews, dating rules and limitations invokes *me*.

"You know, I can't go. My mother said . . ."

Then I imagine him sheepishly ratting me out. I know he doesn't mean to. He just can't hold privileged information. The boy can't hold water.

I discuss that with him.

"Son, you cannot do that. If I am having a conversation with you, I am having it with *you*. Not with anybody else. Not with you and a girl who's hanging around you, wanting to spend time with you. Not with you and one of your friends. With *you*. Just you. Are we clear?"

"We're clear."

"Good. I don't want to run into a problem."

"There won't be any problem."

Then we come to the Homecoming Dance.

Problem.

I'll call her Carla.

I see her at the concession stand at one of Stephen's games. I've seen Carla before, at other games, milling about, and now I understand why. She obviously has an interest in Stephen. I can see why he would be interested in her. She's pretty. Very pretty. I have to give her that. And perky. I'm not so crazy about perky. Especially around my recently turned sixteen-year-old son. I can tell by looking at her and I know by asking around—she's also older. Seventeen.

At this game, on a weekend, I see Carla moving toward me at the concession stand to get a drink. I'm standing in front of her. I decide to break the ice and say hello.

"Hey," I say, smiling, friendly. "How are you?"

Carla ignores me. Doesn't respond to my greeting.

Now, she knows who I am. She knows I'm Stephen's mom.

The strict mom.

That doesn't matter.

She's disrespectful to me. She's cold. She's rude.

If I'm being honest—and I am—the first words that come into my head are—

I know you're seventeen, but I will kill you.

That's my mother, Candy, coming out, the badass making a guest appearance.

I try to slap that down.

I go back to our seats, and I tell Dell about our noninteraction.

"I think you're reading too much into it," he says. "She probably didn't hear you."

"Oh, please, she heard me. I spoke right to her."

Dell sighs.

I seethe.

After the game, I do my due diligence. I ask some people I know about Carla. Everyone tells me what I already know.

"Oh, she thinks she's the bomb."

"She's very, very pretty," I say.

"Yeah, she knows it, too."

And she has designs on my son.

I don't say that out loud. I don't have to.

The next night, Stephen drops his own bomb.

"So, Mom, I wanted to ask you something. It's about Homecoming."

"What about it?"

"I want to go. And—I want to ask a girl. I want to ask this girl Carla."

I try to keep my anger bottled up, but I'm burning inside and some of the steam boils up and shoots out.

"First of all, y'all—"

I exhale, start again.

"You—*you*—are not going to go with any girls right now. *But.* If y'all want to go, I am going to let you go—so don't press me about taking a *date*."

"Well, Mom—"

"I'm still going to let you go, but do not think you are going to pull something over on me and tell me you all are going with a bunch of guys because I know you are not. Don't tell me that's what you're going to do and then try to sneak around and finagle things and meet up with Carla at the dance. I believe that is what you are thinking. And you know what? That is not happening. And furthermore—"

I'm really revving up now. I'm so wound up I have to exhale to allow the rest of my breath to explode.

"I don't want to hear that you are actually taking her. I will hear that. You know I will. Because here's the thing."

I lower my voice to allow Stephen to concentrate fully on what I'm about to say. He stares at me, wide-eyed, both amazed at my rant and a little bit scared.

"Anybody that my children associate with—anyone who becomes their friend and eventually anybody who becomes more, *in the future*—I will embrace that person two hundred percent. But Carla would not be my first choice for you. She's too old and she's not a good—*fit*."

Stephen says nothing and I think I've said too much. I take another deep breath and leave it at that. Stephen knows how I feel. And I know Stephen. He's heard me and he won't give up.

Two days later, while we're cleaning up after dinner, the telephone rings.

Seth leaves the room, answers it, and comes back into the kitchen.

"Mom. Phone."

"Who is it?"

He shrugs. "A girl."

"She wants to talk to me?"

He shrugs again. "That's what she said."

I look at him, then at Stephen, who conveniently has his back turned as he carries some dishes over to the sink. I take the phone from Seth. "Hello?"

"Hey, Mrs. Curry."

A young woman's voice. A voice I don't know. But I can guess.

"Hi," I say. "Who is this?"

"It's Carla."

I pause. "Yes?"

"Well, I was talking to Stephen and he told me that you weren't going to let him go to the dance with me because—"

Carla laughs uncomfortably, composes herself, and continues.

"Because I wouldn't, you know, I mean I *didn't* speak to you at the game."

I look at Stephen. He tries to pretend that he has no idea what's going on. I look at Seth. He gives me the same look. The two of them, playing dumb.

Yeah.

That's not working.

I lock eyes with Stephen. He freezes my stare. He won't back down. Then I stare at Seth. I know he can read what I'm saying without speaking. He pretends he has a problem with something on his shirt.

So you're in on it, too. You agreed to take the call.

"Baby," I say to Carla on the phone, "I'm really, really pissed at my sons right now. I haven't said anything to them. Yet. But they're staring at me and I am letting them know with my eyes that I am pissed off."

I pause again. I hear Carla breathing. I pace, curl the phone cord between my fingers. I'm thinking strangulation. I drop the cord and I say—

"Let's put all that aside. Now, Carla, since you are calling me, let me say, yes, I was very disappointed in the way you acted toward me."

"Well, that's why I'm calling. I want to apologize."

I look back at Stephen. He's dying to know what Carla has said. He knows what she's *supposed* to say. He knows because he orchestrated this entire phone call. Devised this dumb plan. I have to give him props for trying. For creativity. For sheer gall.

"Babe," I say to Carla. "I appreciate your apology."

I look at Stephen again. He exhales with relief. I can see that he thinks this is going well, all according to his plan.

"But, Carla," I say, "you are only apologizing to me now because y'all are trying to get this together."

Stephen doesn't move an inch, but I can feel his spirits sink.

"And, Carla, I'm going to tell you—and I know Stephen already told you—that he wasn't supposed to go to the dance with you anyway. And if y'all think you are boyfriend and girlfriend? No. That's a hard no. He is not going to have a girlfriend right now."

I look at the phone in my hand. I start to speak to Carla again, but no words come. Instead, I hear this thought in my head.

This isn't about you, Carla, I think. *This is about how I'm trying to raise my son. It's all about him. My son. How I am trying to guide him through every kind of situation. All situations.*

Then to my shock, I feel myself starting to break. I begin feeling emotional and defiant at the same time.

My son, I think. *I am trying to help my son.*

I look at Stephen, staring at me with such expectation, and then I look at Seth, staring at me with curiosity, and I am filled up. I feel my eyes begin to tear.

My *sons.*

I have to protect my sons.

Until it comes time that I can't. They will have to protect themselves.

I'm trying to . . . guide my son, I say to myself, and then I say to Carla aloud, "Carla, I'm sorry y'all can't go to the dance together."

"Okay," Carla says, quietly.

I laugh to cover the residue of emotion that still clings. I turn away from the boys and flick at a droplet I feel on my cheek.

"Hopefully, Carla, next time I see you, we can speak to each other."

"We will, Mrs. Curry. I promise."

"We good now?" I ask.

"Yes."

"Okay, then, bye."

I hang up the phone and whirl on Stephen. "I cannot believe that you would get her to do this. You put her up to this."

"I thought—"

"You *thought?*"

I stare through him.

"So, I mean, the dance—"

"Just be glad that I'm not changing my mind. Yes. I keep my promises. I'm still letting y'all go to the dance."

"Wow. Great. Thanks."

This is too much. I wave my hand in front of my face. "Go. Go upstairs. Just go."

He sprints upstairs, Seth a step behind him. I want to shout to him, *I didn't tell you to go*, but I let them both go. Seth. His co-conspirator.

I need to compose myself. I crash down at the kitchen table, bury my head in my hands.

How old is Sydel? I ask myself. *Nine? She won't be going off to college for another* nine *years?*

Nine more years.

I'm abstaining from alcohol now, but the day I drop her off at her dorm, I am coming home and pouring myself a huge glass of wine.

17

Live Your Life

Have I not commanded you? Be strong and courageous. Do not
be afraid; do not be discouraged, for the Lord your God will be
with you wherever you go.

—Joshua 1:9

"BE YOUR own man. Live your life."

Seth's motto.

Seth has begun high school and has become more private, keeping his thoughts to himself and his communication to a minimum. When he does talk, he speaks in short bursts, no fluff, no couching his words. He speaks directly and to the point. Sometimes he's so direct, his words cut.

I call him on it. "Son, dang, why did you have to say it like that?"

He shrugs.

He shrugs a lot.

"I don't know any other way to say it."

I have to give him props for being honest, for being real.

In school, he does just enough to get by. This irritates me because I know how smart he is. I know he could excel. He simply refuses to push himself. I pray about that, concerned that he'll need to put in more effort to get by in life. We talk about that. Or at least I do.

"Seth, if you put in just thirty more minutes a night on your homework, you could make straight As."

He shrugs. "Why would I want to do that?"

I'm stunned by his reaction.

"Are you kidding me?" I say. "Did those words really come out of your mouth?"

But I know him. I know that I can't force him into anything. He has to come to his own decisions and choices, at his own time. When we talk about his future, even vaguely, he says, "Mom, that's your goal for me. That's not my goal."

I want to argue with him about putting in more effort, but I don't. I can only laugh. And then *I* shrug.

"Okay," I say. "If you're telling me that putting in the time and effort isn't important to you in order for you to excel, then I can only say that I hope this doesn't come back and bite you in the butt. Because I have a feeling that it will."

He doesn't say anything. So I wrap it up.

"I know you hear me, but I want you to remember this conversation later, when you're in college and when you're out in the real world."

"Okay. Can I go now?"

"Go ahead."

As he goes, I shake my head.

My son. He is his own man. He is true to himself. I'll give him that.

He does exasperate me. At one point, he becomes a handful. He falls into a period of extreme mumbling and talking back. I feel myself losing control over it. I pray about it. I meditate in the prayer closet. I wake up dreaming about it, then I prayer walk into his room and pray over him. Then I try to talk to him, but he won't let me get a word out.

"Son—Seth—can I just say something to you and you don't debate me? You don't argue with me? I look at you and the way you argue and debate and I swear you have all the makings of a world-famous trial lawyer."

He keeps debating me. He keeps talking back. I lock myself in the closet for two hours and I pray. I leaf through the Bible and I look up every verse that pertains to "tongues." I read from Psalm 141:3: "Set a guard over my mouth, Lord; keep watch over the door of my lips."

That night, I repeat that verse over Seth as he sleeps.

The next day, I find another verse, from Proverbs 10:19.

"Sin is not ended by multiplying words, but the prudent hold their tongues."

I show that one to Seth and this one from Proverbs 21:23 and have him read them both aloud:

"Those who guard their mouths and their tongues keep themselves from calamity."

He looks up at me and rolls his eyes.

"Do you understand that?" I ask him. "I'm trying to keep you from *calamity*."

One night, we get into it. I don't remember the reason or the subject or situation, but I lose it. *I am done with this*, I think. I have just finished having him repeat a short verse from Psalm 52:4: "You love every harmful word, you deceitful tongue."

"What does that even mean?" Seth asks, dismissing it with an attitude.

"What does it *mean*?" I shout. "It means don't talk back to me. You have to hold your *tongue*."

He shrugs and murmurs, "If you say so."

That does it.

I'm completely irrational.

I call Dell on the phone.

"I've had it," I say. "You better get here and pick up *your* son."

"Pick up my son? I'm in Toronto. It's eleven o'clock at night. What do you want me to do?"

"I DON'T KNOW."

"Sonya—"

"I am about to lose whatever I have left of my *mind*."

"I can't leave the team and fly home for this."

"I know, I know, I know."

Wow, I think. *I sure picked the wrong fourteen years to give up drinking.*

I glare at Seth and then I hiss at Dell over the phone. "I'll handle it."

"Okay. Good."

I hang up the phone. I turn to Seth. I feel my lips tighten and my eyes narrow. I look at Seth as if I'm looking through flames.

"Mom," Seth says.

He sees that something has gone—off. The look on my face. My eerily level voice. The charge of electricity shooting through my body.

"I guess I'm going to go—"

He starts to stand up.

"Sit down."

Now he can see that I'm furious. Beyond furious. Nervously, he takes a seat across the table from me. I start to pace. He follows me with his eyes. I whip around and stare at him. He lowers his eyes. I keep pacing. I stop and reach inside a drawer. My fingers curl around a plastic tube. I take out the tube and shut the drawer with my hip. I can't believe that I am even considering what I am about to do. But I have come to the end.

Seth looks up at me. He senses—danger.

"What are you going to do?"

"Don't. Talk. To. Me."

I take a deep breath and exhale like I'm blowing out a cake with fifty burning candles.

"If you say one more thing—*one more thing*—I am going to superglue your lips together."

"You—*what?*"

"You heard me."

He cracks up. "Yeah, right, like you would ever do that. That's child abuse. I saw an episode of *Law and Order*—"

My son has no idea how fast I can move.

Before he has a moment to react, I'm on him, squeezing the tube, plopping the superglue onto his lips. Seth jerks his head away and only a few drops land.

"What THE—?"

I start shaking. I look at the superglue in my hand and drop it on the counter like it's a loaded gun.

"It's gone. I've lost my mind," I say.

"My wips aw stuck togevah," Seth says.

"Really?"

"Reweee!"

"I am so sorry," I say, first in genuine horror and in fear for what I have done to my own child, and then—I can't help myself—I burst out laughing.

"I can't believe I just did that." I look at the superglue as if noticing it for the first time and then I say, "You made Candy come out of me. I channeled your grandma. I felt so *badass*."

Seth and I stare at each other. We don't speak. I focus on the two drops of superglue that have pooled up on his bottom lip. I dab at them. They have become tiny, rock-hard mounds.

"Really hard," I say, and then we both start laughing. We explode into hysterics, laughing so hard that we cry. Finally, our laughter stops and Seth picks at the superglue hilltops on his lip. Miserably, he scratches at one, taking off a tiny piece of skin.

"Ow," he says.

"I really am sorry," I say, but I feel myself starting to crack up again.

He shakes his head.

"You should've stopped at the Scwiptures," he mutters, scratching off another piece of skin from his lip.

Sophomore year of high school.

Seth wants to change schools.

"I want to transfer out of Charlotte Christian," he says.

We sit together in the kitchen. I lean both my arms onto the counter. "Where do you want to go?"

He shrugs. He's buying time. I know him. He's thought this through. I know he has a high school in mind. He mentions the school. A local basketball powerhouse.

"Why?" I ask.

"They have a better basketball team. We'd have a good chance of winning a state championship. I want to win. Charlotte Christian is—"

He stops, holds, and then says, "You know."

"No, I don't know. I'm not sure what you're driving at. What are you actually saying?"

"Not as good," he says.

I don't say anything. But I know that Seth has an issue with being in his brother's shadow at his current high school. Sometimes I think he wears it like a coat. I know he wants to wriggle free from it and find his own light.

Be your own man.

Seth lives by that creed. I understand. I can't argue with him. This other high school does have a superior basketball program. But is it the better place for him, for our family? That's how I look at it. This school wouldn't just be getting Seth. They'll be getting our family. Will our values match?

"I think it would be a better fit for me," Seth says.

"Well," I say. "All right."

Seth nearly shoots out of his chair.

"All *right*?"

"All right, I'll look into it," I say.

"Okay," Seth says, standing. "Thanks."

I do look into it. Dell and I both do. We check out the coaches, the facilities, the classrooms, the teachers, and we talk about whether Seth should transfer. We list the pros and cons. And of course, I pray about it. I ask for guidance. Eventually something clicks in a dream. I awake knowing. I see the path forward. One day, I sit Seth back down in the kitchen.

"I can't go with it, Seth," I say. "I can't go along with you transferring."

Seth blurts, "Why do I always have to do everything Stephen does?"

"It's not about that."

Seth goes quiet, mumbles something.

"I want to explain. I owe that to you and I want you to understand. Right now, it is my responsibility to parent you. You are my responsibility."

"I know," he says.

"I take that responsibility seriously. Seriously like you wouldn't believe. It is my responsibility to put you into an environment that I feel promotes and supports you—as a *human being.*"

"This school is better for basketball," he says.

"I can't argue with that," I say. "You're right."

He looks at me.

"I totally get that you want to be your own person. That should be everyone's goal, to stand on their own two feet, to make their own mark. But you have to understand this. Given the choice—seeing how we fit, how our family fits—Charlotte Christian is where you should be. You know why?"

"Why?"

"Because it's not about basketball. I'm going to say something that you may not believe, but you have to try."

I pause and then I say, "I don't care about basketball."

Seth stares at me as if I've spoken in a foreign language.

"It's true. I know. Your dad's an NBA player. Our world revolves around basketball. It's the family business. But only two percent of college players actually make it to the NBA. Two out of every hundred. Beyond that, I care about *you.* As a person. So if you want to go to this other school because of basketball, that's a hard no. I am rearing you to be grounded, an independent person, a godly person. I don't care if you're a basketball player."

I lean back in my chair and watch my son watching me. I do

believe I can read his thoughts. I'm not sure I want to read his thoughts right now.

"Do you understand?" I ask.

"I understand," he says.

"But you don't agree."

"I don't really have a choice, do I?"

"Well," I say. "No."

I reach over and put my hand over his. He seems shocked, but he doesn't pull away.

"I know you're frustrated," I say. "I know that. I understand that you want to be in a stronger program. We just can't do that. So, let's change the perspective. Let's be positive. What *can* you do?"

"At Charlotte Christian," he says, his voice level, resigned.

"Yes," I say. "At Charlotte Christian. You have to look at it as a challenge. Get in there and contribute. Make a difference. *Be* the difference. Don't run from the challenge. Take it on."

"Make the best of it," he says without much enthusiasm.

"Exactly."

"Can I go now?"

"Yes. You can go."

"Tzuh," he says.

He gets up from the table and starts to leave the kitchen. He hesitates at the door. He turns back and opens his mouth slightly as if he is about to say something. I pretend to know what he's going to say.

Thanks, Mom. I appreciate you hearing me out and that you at least considered the idea of me transferring.

He doesn't say that. He wouldn't.

I do believe that's what he feels in his heart.

Well, that's what I want to believe.

He doesn't say anything, but I'm pretty sure that what he really intended to say was, *Life isn't fair.*

We do supplement Seth's basketball in high school. In addition to playing for Charlotte Christian, he joins one of the area's top travel teams. He quickly discovers that the travel team plays against tougher competition than his high school team. He rises to the challenge and becomes one of the best players on his team. As Seth enters junior year of high school, coaches from Division I colleges take notice. They start coming to Seth's games. A buzz starts building. Seth Curry has it all. He can shoot, score, pass, and plays solid defense. Some of these same coaches missed out on Stephen. They thought he was too scrawny and wouldn't survive the rough play of Division I. Two years later, Stephen, a junior at Davidson College, the only Division I team that wanted him, leads the country in scoring. These coaches don't want to make that same mistake with Seth.

At the end of the school year, Seth's travel team will play in a prestigious national tournament. The Who's Who of college coaches will fill the stands and scout the best players, among them Seth. The prize? Perhaps an invitation to join a highly ranked Division I basketball program. I hear that coaches from Duke, Kentucky, Kansas will attend. We sign Seth up, make all the arrangements. One slight glitch. The tournament begins the day after Seth's senior prom.

We talk curfew.

"I know it's prom night," I say. "So let's figure this out."

He panics. "I'm going to prom, right?"

"Yes. Of course. We would never take that away from you. Now, here's the thing. We have to leave for the airport first thing in the morning. You have to be up and ready to roll at seven."

"What time's my curfew?"

"I was going to say one—"

He looks shocked. "One o'clock on prom night?"

I shift in my chair. "I was *going* to say one—I'd like you to be home at one—but I understand. It's prom. So we're going to make your curfew two o'clock."

He tries that out. "Two o'clock."

"Sharp."

He nods, says nothing, mumbles something.

"Seth, this is an important tournament. You've got coaches coming from all over the country to see you. You need to be rested and ready to go. We're going to go with two o'clock. I feel that's more than fair."

"Okay."

I pause. Look him in the eye. I start to speak, hold my tongue.

"*Okay*," he repeats, which, translated, I understand to mean, *Like I have any choice.*

"Be sure you're all packed. That way we can hustle out of here."

"I'll be packed," he says and heads off to his room.

We have different views of the future, I realize. I'm planning the next four years and beyond. He's planning the next twenty-four hours.

Prom night.

Two in the morning.

We wait, Dell and I, camped out on the couch in the living room, all the lights on, the two of us forming a cartoon tableau cliché from every high school movie—the nervous parents waiting up for their kid to come home from the party. Or, in this case, the prom. Dell clicks through TV channels with the remote. I flip through a magazine.

Two fifteen.

"He's late," I say, stating the obvious, but also embracing the forgivable. It's senior prom. I can allow fifteen minutes. I'll huff and puff but I'll accept it. But I'm not sure I can allow much more.

Two thirty.

Dell says nothing but surfs through the channels with a vengeance. An old detective movie. A rerun of a seventies' sitcom. The shopping channel. *SportsCenter.* I've long given up on the magazine. I stare at the TV, my eyes glazed over, my patience frayed to a thread, my anger rising.

Two forty-five.

No Seth.

I look at Dell. He doesn't look back. I bite my lip. I feel the anger burning in my stomach like acid. I am now officially pissed. Beyond pissed. Even worse, I feel disrespected. I feel played.

Two fifty-nine. Three a.m. Three ten. Three fifteen . . .

The jingling of a key in the front door.

The door opens.

Seth walks in, closes the door behind him. He turns and sees us. Startled, he freezes for half a second. He composes himself, nods, and tries on a smile. "What's up?"

He waves at us, grins, and heads up to his room, taking the stairs two at a time.

My blood boils. I feel as if I am on fire. I look at Dell.

"You saw that, right?"

"Yeah."

"You just saw what I saw."

Not a question. A fact. An accusation.

I stand, pace away from the couch, turn back to Dell. I lower my voice, tamping down the fire that's now raging throughout me and I say, my voice trembling in anger. "I'm glad you saw the same thing I saw. Now go upstairs and get him right now."

I don't see Dell take the stairs. I keep my back to the staircase. I hear a door knock, a door opening, muffled voices, footsteps descending the stairs. Dell enters the living room, stands to my side. I turn and face Seth. He stands at the bottom of the stairs, his eyes wide. I look him over. I don't speak for a long time. I just stare at him.

"What?" he says finally. "What?"

"You know that tournament? That extremely important tournament? Guess what?"

No one speaks.

I take a step toward Seth.

"You're not going. We were supposed to leave for the airport in a few hours. I will not put you on a flight in your condition."

"My—"

"You're not going to get any sleep. You won't be rested at all. I am not going to allow you to get on a plane, go to that tournament, and embarrass yourself in front of all those coaches who have come specifically to see you. You're not ready."

Seth lowers his head, slightly. I wave my hand.

"And that's not even the point," I say. "The point is that you did not have enough control over your actions or respect for us to come home when we told you—when we agreed. Your head is not on right. We made an agreement. We made a deal. You could go to prom and you could go to the tournament as long as you came home by your curfew. Your curfew is long past. You're not going."

He shrugs. "Okay."

He turns and goes back upstairs.

I look at Dell.

"I don't think he believes me," I say.

The next morning, at the time we are to leave for the airport, I sit in my robe, sipping coffee at the kitchen table. I hear footsteps coming down the stairs. I look up and see Seth standing in the doorway, his backpack slung over his shoulder.

"I'm ready," he says.

"For what?"

"The tournament."

I tilt my head and feel my mouth drop open. "Seth, did you think I was kidding? You thought I was playing?" I exhale, look away for a moment, then turn back to him, my voice low. "Son, do you remember the talk we had a while ago? I told you that I don't care about basketball."

I put my coffee cup down so hard on the table that the cup rattles. The noise jars Seth. He winces.

"Let me repeat what I said then," I say. "I don't care about basketball. You know what I care about? You. As a person. I care about the kind of person that you are and the person you become. And if you are going to disrespect your parents . . . ?"

I shake my head.

"I can't allow that."

I start to speak, feel my throat catch, and then I whisper with a passion I don't expect, "You are also disrespecting the opportunity that God has given you. You can do that when you're not in our household. But right now, you can't do that. You can't. Seth—"

He takes one step toward me, stops. He seems unsure of what to do, of where to be.

"The thing is . . ." I say.

I swallow. I feel tears starting to form. I try to bat them back.

"I am going to continue to pray about this. I know that God's will is going to be done in your life because He created you for something. At this point, do I know if that is basketball? I don't. I really don't know. That is the least of my worries. The *least* of my worries. I want to know that I am raising a decent human being."

"Okay," Seth says.

He wants out of there, out of the kitchen and away from me.

He turns away. He mumbles something on his way out of the kitchen. He trudges up the stairs, slowly, heavily. I hear his door close not with a slam, but firmly, with finality. He will avoid me as much as possible during the rest of the weekend. He will say little. It will take time—weeks, maybe more—but he will eventually bounce back, returning to the Seth I know, ultimately accepting my decision because as I'm sure he would say, *What choice do I have?*

My decision.

My decision not to allow my son to go to a basketball tournament that he has been counting on for months. The most important tournament of his life.

Feeling exhausted, my body aching, I push myself from the table, move to the counter, pour myself another cup of coffee, and sit back down. I stare off, scanning the large open room, taking in details of the kitchen, my eyes settling on the whiteboard. I focus on the color-coded symbols of my children, their favorite colors instead of their names, listing their chores for the week, above, below, and to the side, Scriptures I've written. I look at Seth's chore for that week: laundry. He has taken on his chore obediently, with no complaints, at least none that I've heard. He contributes to the family. He does his part to keep the Big Machine running at peak capacity.

My decision.

I feel my legs shake.

"Crap," I murmur. "Did I just mess him up? Did I just mess up his *life*? Oh, Lord, should he have gone?"

I wrap both hands around my coffee cup, feel the warmth pulse through my fingers, and, in my mind, I say to Seth, *Well, son, if I did, I am truly sorry. I feel terrible. I really do.*

I look up then, vaguely contemplate the ceiling, and whisper into the air, "My decision. Do I have second thoughts about my decision?"

I return my gaze to my coffee cup.

"No," I say, "I don't. Not one second thought. Not a shred of doubt."

I know this with all my heart. If God gave me the opportunity to repeat the previous night, I would do exactly the same thing. And I would feel as terrible as I do right now.

As hard as it was, as awful as I feel, I know I made the right decision.

For Seth.

18

Bar Mitzvah

WHEN SPRING comes and the weather improves and the temperatures rise, we begin our weekly outdoor ritual: cookouts. To some, a "cookout" conjures a sedate, backyard get-together, a few people talking, sipping beers, a dad—usually—off to one side, grilling hot dogs, burgers, and buns. On the other side, a few kids scamper on the lawn or splash around in the pool. Your typical cookout.

Not close to our cookouts.

Our cookouts are legendary. Each one is an *event*. An extravagant open house packed with people, enough food to feed an army, wall-to-wall activities, music, laughter, games. A once-a-year indoor/outdoor party that we hold every week.

We start by bringing our weekend card games outside. In our family, we *play*. Board games. Card games. We play seriously. We play for fun. And—no surprise—we play to win. We usually play Spades or a dice game called Left, Right, Center. We always play for money. We play to win and we roar with laughter. When we bring out the board games, we often go first to Pokeno, a variation of Bingo that, yes, we play for money. We also play Life and of course Monopoly, which is a game I don't love. It seems so random. Where you land determines your fate. I suppose that's like life. I find the game too slow and too long. And I usually lose.

For our cookouts, we invite close friends and family, the number, including kids, sometimes ballooning to fifty people or even more. We blare music over our outdoor speaker system. We swim in the pool. We play pickup basketball or games of H-O-R-S-E. People play Ping-Pong downstairs or pool upstairs. Sometimes, depending on the occasion, perhaps July Fourth or somebody's birthday, we have the cookouts catered. Usually we ourselves cook, grilling burgers and hot dogs. Everyone contributes—salads, side dishes, desserts, and people bring their own beer, wine, or hard liquor. I'm still on my alcohol hiatus, but I don't restrict others from imbibing.

We don't start the cookouts at a set time. People usually start arriving at two or three in the afternoon. We don't have a cutoff time. You come over anytime you want and leave whenever you feel like it. Typically, people stay until two in the morning. I totally get it. Why would anyone want to leave a Curry cookout? I move through the house, outside, inside, engaging, playing, supervising, monitoring, checking that all is running smoothly. The food keeps coming and the beverages keep flowing. Sometimes, I'll pause in a doorway or stop outside by the basketball court or the pool and just watch and listen. I hear contentment. I hear love. I hear joy. Everyone here seems relaxed, comfortable, free from the trials of their week, letting loose, having a blast. I know this may sound strange, but sometimes I close my eyes and think—

This is it. This is what I always wanted in a family. What I see—what I feel here, right now—is holy.

When the kids graduate from high school, I put together videos for them. I pull photographs from family albums and newspaper clippings from local media that we've collected and saved. I also incorporate music. Songs the kids like. Songs I like, including gospel music. And I put in my favorite song. I find myself constantly going back to a song by Lee Ann Womack called "I Hope You Dance." The song speaks to me as a mom. I have practically memorized all the lyrics. I've written snatches of the lyrics all over the house, mainly on the walls in their rooms and playrooms. The lyrics stay lodged in my head, a mantra, an inspiration, a prayer—"I hope you never lose your sense of wonder" and "May you never take one single breath for granted." I think of "I Hope You Dance" as our family's theme song. I score Stephen's and Seth's video using the song. Eventually, Sydel will choose the song for her wedding.

As part of Stephen's and Seth's high school graduation celebrations, I decide to give them my version of a bar mitzvah. I have always been intrigued by the history of the Jews and I have been fascinated by the Hebrew language. I've begun taking courses in Hebrew and have studied the transition from the Old Testament to the New Testament. I value the richness of story and feel in awe of the rigor of God in the Old Testament. It helps underscore the beauty I find in the New Testament.

I schedule the boys' bar mitzvahs during a cookout on a Saturday in June. I plan that we'll have the ceremony first and then, as with most bar mitzvahs, we'll party. I buy Stephen and Seth prayer shawls and I purchase a simple, user-friendly book of traditional prayers and songs. I invite all our family, friends, and Stephen's and Seth's friends to attend and to participate in the joint event.

The bar mitzvah starts in late afternoon, as the light of the day fades. Stephen and Seth drape their prayer shawls around their shoulders and bow their heads as the officiant reads and recites a prayer. He speaks to them together and then says something to each of them individually. He offers words of wisdom and guidance and presents them with a direction to move forward in their lives, a path of love, generosity, and righteousness. He asks them to bow their heads. He prays over each of them, blessing them. Then he asks if anyone in attendance wants to say anything. Many of our friends and family speak. Finally, I speak. I ask the boys to appreciate the gifts they have been given athletically and materially. I ask that they keep themselves humble, even as they walk through their lives with confidence and pride. I ask them to remember this day and to keep the love they feel from this gathering in their hearts. I implore them to keep God in their hearts. And I ask them to begin every day with faith. I try not to cry. I can't help it. I do.

Then someone shouts, "Mazel tov!" and in the tradition of all good bar mitzvahs, we eat well and party deep into the night.

19

Hero of My Own Story

Do not be anxious about anything, but in every situation,
by prayer and petition, with thanksgiving, present your requests
to God.

—*Philippians 4:6*

JUNE 15, 1994.

I'm pregnant, at the midway point, the baby due in early October. We've chosen not to find out the gender. Unlike Stephen and Seth, we planned this pregnancy. We've decided that we want a third child and we want a girl.

"Let's mix it up," we say. "Add some balance."

The evening after a visit with my doctor, as we sit in the living room, I start to panic. I feel myself flush and my hands start to tremble.

"Dell, I'm shaking," I say. "I'm feeling really anxious. I think I'm having a panic attack."

I spin and face him. I don't shout, but I hear my voice hit a higher register, and I blurt, "I don't want a girl."

"What?"

"I can't have a girl, Dell."

He blinks, confused. "I thought having a girl was the whole point of getting pregnant again."

"I'm too much of a tomboy. What will I do with her?"

He studies me, incredulous, his mouth hanging open. A quiet man in general, he has been rendered completely mute.

"What if she loves the color pink and frilly clothes and she wants to do girly things like go to ballet class or dancing or—I don't know—what do girls even *do*?"

"I'm not sure. I don't really—"

"I don't like those things. And I'm not, you know—"

I stop myself. I don't really want to say what I'm thinking.

"What?" Dell says.

"Nothing."

"What? Tell me."

"I'm not fuzzy or warm or touchy-feely. I've always hung out with guys. I know guys. I get them. They're easy. I'm comfortable around them. Look around here. What do you see?"

Dell takes a shot. "Guys?"

"Exactly. Me. And guys."

I gesture wildly. "What if she's emotional? Or sensitive? I'm not sensitive. Dell, I will ruin her life."

"You're sensitive, Sonya."

"I am not. You know I'm not."

"You can be."

"I don't have the right mentality for a girl."

"We don't even know if we're having a girl."

"*I* know. I know it's a girl. I can tell. This girl is already causing me problems." I sigh. "This conversation can't be helping."

"You're going to be great. And you are sensitive."

"I am *not*."

On October 10, I give birth to our daughter, Sydel Alicia Curry. The nurse cleans her up, swathes her, and puts her in my arms. I look at her and I melt. I fall so deeply in love with her that tears flow down my cheeks.

"God," I say. "I am so thankful for this girl. You are exactly who I want."

I kiss her tiny scrunched-up forehead. Love pours out of me, bathes her like a shower.

"Sydel," I say to her, tapping her tiny nose. "My baby girl."

Even as a toddler, Sydel brings a kind of fire into our family. High energy. Spunk. Spirit. She's smart and sassy. She keeps up with the boys. At the same time, she's all girl. Eventually, she will go through her ballet phase and falling in love with the color pink phase, and a frilly fashion phase. She's so cute about all of it that I melt more than when I first saw her. She also brings nurturing and caring and love—outward, demonstrative—love into the family. When you least expect it, Sydel will throw her arms around you and hug you with all her might. Or she'll surprise you by coming over to you suddenly and rubbing your head. Of course, later, when she gets older, she'll get into sports. She'll excel at softball, basketball, and volleyball and while I never say this aloud, she may be the best athlete in the family. Even later, when she gets older, we'll enter a new phase together. Sydel and I will become shopping buddies, traveling pals, my moviegoing partner, my constant companion.

My best friend.

. . .

Sydel is five.

She has been moody, acting up, defying me, testing me. She needs a break. I need a break. After she blatantly disobeys me, I send her to her room. She storms upstairs, slams the door. Inside her room, her temper flares, ignites. I hear a crash, screaming, the sound of banging as something hits the floor, shatters. I run upstairs and fling open her door. She has trashed her room, torpedoed everything—toys, dolls, stuffed animals, clothes, books. In a rage, a whirlwind, she rips through every piece of clothing in her closet, lobbing armfuls of pants, shorts, shirts, dresses onto the floor. She yanks open her dresser and empties a drawerful of underwear. She shows no sign of stopping.

I race downstairs and call Dell, who is on the road. From down here, on the phone, I can hear even more destruction and freaking out coming from upstairs.

"Your daughter just tore up her room," I tell Dell.

"What?"

"I sent her to her room because she disobeyed me, and she just lost it. She's thrown all her clothes, toys, everything, onto the floor. And she's screaming."

"What are you going to do?"

"I don't know."

But I do know.

Montessori is about to intersect with my home life.

A natural consequence, I think. *The goal.*

I hang up with Dell and grab an entire box of black plastic trash bags. I wade into the destruction, a sea of clothes, toys, dolls, and photo albums covering the floor. Sydel hugs herself in the corner, panting, exhausted. I open a trash bag and start stuffing it with her toys. I fill one bag, then another, then start shoving clothes into a third trash bag. Sydel watches me, riveted, uncertain, amazed, wondering—*What is she doing?*

"You sure have a lot of stuff," I say, tying a trash bag, beginning to fill up another. I intend this statement for Sydel, but it feels like a realization to me. How did she accumulate so much? Did we buy her all these—things? Meanwhile, Sydel stays frozen in the corner, her arms locked around herself.

I finish filling a fourth trash bag, and then I pick out five pairs of her pants, five shirts, five changes of underwear, and then I go into her bathroom and collect her toothbrush, toothpaste, and soap. When I come back into her room, she starts to cry, softly. Her outrage has fizzled, replaced now by fear. She has no idea what I am doing but she knows she's not going to like it.

"When you finish your temper tantrum," I say, "and you can listen to my words, I'll explain what just happened and what I'm doing."

Sydel sniffles, swipes at her tears, nods. She draws herself up, exhales. I can see that she wants to know where she stands, how this ends.

"What a mess," I say under my breath, scanning the room, thinking, *How in the world can this little person—this five-year-old—do so much damage in such a short time?*

I look at her. She's calm. For the moment. But she's watching me with suspicion, her eyes focused like searchlights, trained on every step I take.

"All right," I say. "Now, Sydel, listen to me carefully. I want you to understand this. I am your mother. I am only required to clothe you, feed you, and protect you. That's as far as it goes. By law. Anything after that? That is a *gift*."

I nod at the five pants, five shirts, and five changes of underwear that I've piled onto her bed.

"That's it. Right there. That's all you're going to get."

She looks at me, her eyes widening, wondering where I'm headed with this, fearing where it may be going.

"Now, because I love you so much, in addition to your clothes, and your toothbrush, I am going to allow you to pick out *one* toy and *one* picture. You can have a toy to play with and I will allow you the one picture so you will have something nice to look at when you come into your room. That's it. You destroyed everything else. Obviously, all your things don't mean anything to you. You threw them away or you broke them. So, okay. You're not going to have any of them."

I wait. Sydel has gone speechless and eerily calm.

After a moment, she walks to a toy she's tossed onto the floor. She picks it up and then she quickly snatches a doll and cradles it.

"Sorry," I say, taking the doll from her. "I said one toy. You can't have the doll."

"I want my doll! Give me my doll! I want my DOLL!"

Sydel collapses to the floor, screaming, kicking, gasping, and then shouting, "DOLL!" whenever she can muster enough breath.

"You want the doll instead?" I ask her.

"Yes!"

"Let go of the toy and I'll give you your doll."

She drops the toy and I hand her the doll. Her favorite. Her deepest attachment. She plays with this doll constantly. She carries it with her everywhere as if the doll is an extra appendage.

"Sydel," I say. "I want you to understand. Do you understand what Mommy is saying?"

She nods, clutching her doll, twisting her body away from me, keeping the doll out of my reach.

"Here's what we're going to do," I say. "If you behave, in two weeks you can start earning your stuff back. I'll allow you to pick another of your toys, or dolls, or games—one at a time. You have to earn everything back."

"Okay," she says in a whisper.

"You understand?"

"Yes."

Slowly, I finish filling the trash bags with her things. Eventually, Sydel rises from the floor, and still clinging to her doll, she helps me put her room back together. We barely speak. Finally, when we've restored her room, I lug the bulging trash bags into our room and stuff them into a closet.

After I haul the last bag out of my daughter's room, I hear myself say, "I will not raise any spoiled kids."

I think about the trash bags filled with all the nice but unnecessary stuff we've bought for her, and I say, "It's too late. I've already spoiled you."

I close the door on the last trash bag and I say, "I've spoiled you, but I don't have to spoil you rotten. That ends now."

It works.

Sydel adjusts her behavior and accepts her punishment—she can take her toys and dolls back every two weeks, one at a time. I watch with fascination as she decides which toy or doll to select. She chooses with thought and care—and over time, through this exercise, this discipline, this training, I believe—I know—that she develops an appreciation for what she has.

As Sydel grows, enters elementary school and then middle school, I watch her evolve into a deep-feeling, empathetic person. She not only feels what those closest to her may be going through, she feels the need to go further, even in some way to get involved. She wants to help. At home, she takes on her brothers' stress, and even my stress. My daughter feels so deeply that I worry about her getting hurt, especially with friends, as she maneuvers her way through the treacherous territory known as the world of teenage girls.

From my perch as head of school, I have a unique vantage point that allows me to observe my daughter daily, but from a distance. I see that she makes friends easily. I wonder if her friends appreciate her empathetic, caring nature. I know how some girls can be and I'm concerned that certain members of her evolving social circle might take advantage of her. After a while, my fears become confirmed. Sydel finds herself bullied and, worse, ignored by one girl in particular whom Sydel identified as her best friend. She comes to me and we talk about what to do. We talk about how to take on bullies, even as they try to harass you. I attempt to teach her a hard lesson—sometimes you have to stand up for yourself, even if you stand alone. We agree that it can be such a narrow tightrope to walk. Being so sensitive, Sydel finds it increasingly impossible to find her footing within the middle school social circle. She comes home not knowing where she will stand the very next day—in with her friends or on the outs. At home, worrying about what the next day will bring, she starts to dread going to school. Finally, in December, halfway through the school year, we both agree that she would benefit from a change of scenery. We arrange for her to transfer to Charlotte Christian to finish middle school and continue on to high school. Her relief is palatable.

On Sydel's first day at Charlotte Christian, some older girls tape her locker shut and cover her locker with obscenities.

We know who they are and it hurts.

They are African Americans and they go to our church.

A great first day, I think.

"Why would they do that?" Sydel, crushed, asks between sobs.

"It's because of who your brothers are," I say. "They don't want you to think you're 'all that.' They're trying to intimidate you."

I shake my head and take in Sydel, my sweet, sensitive daughter, the least stuck-up kid you could imagine. My heart breaks for her.

"It's so ridiculous," she says.

"It's outrageous," I say. "Now the question is, what do you want to do about it?"

She balls up a tissue and dabs at her eyes. "I don't know."

"Well, you're going to have to figure it out. If you want to address these girls but you don't feel safe talking to them directly, face-to-face, alone, I can help you with a strategy."

"I want to face them," she says immediately and with determination.

"Good. That's what I want you to do."

"I have to stand up for myself."

I smile at her. "Exactly. We are not going to be those parents who are always running to the school and fighting your battles. You have to learn how to fight them yourself."

"What do I do?"

"Well, here's one idea. Go to the principal yourself and talk to her. Tell her what happened."

Sydel nods, takes this in.

"Are you comfortable with that?" I ask.

"Yes."

The next day, Sydel meets with the principal and explains what happened. The principal reacts appropriately. She calls in the girls who trashed Sydel's locker and disciplines them. Sydel feels proud of herself and I'm proud of her.

"You did the right thing," I say. "You stood up for yourself at school."

"I felt empowered," she says.

"Good." I smile. "And now I'm going to show you what we're going to do *outside* of school."

Sydel perks up. "What do you mean?"

"I know the mom of the main girl. The ringleader. I would like the two of us to speak with the mom and her daughter after church one day. Would you be comfortable with that?"

"Oh, yeah," Sydel says, and grins. "Are we talking about revenge?"

"No," I say. "Justice."

Mom to mom.

That's how this is going down.

One on one.

As a Christian, I have learned that when someone wrongs you, you must go to that person and speak with them face-to-face. If that doesn't work, only then should you seek the help of someone higher up. And so, after church one day, I locate the mother of the girl—the ringleader—and ask if my daughter and I can speak to her and her daughter. I bring Sydel over and we all step to the side.

After introductions, I say, "Are you aware of what happened at school this week?"

"No," the mom says.

"You don't know what your daughter did?"

"I have no idea."

I explain about the girls taping over Sydel's locker on her first day at Charlotte Christian. I describe how crushed Sydel felt.

And then I say, "I'm not here to fight my daughter's battles, but I want to share with you that as a mom, I'm very disappointed. First, I'm disappointed as a Christian. Your daughter and these other girls did this for no reason. They were not provoked in any way. They just lashed out. I believe they wanted to make some kind of statement to my daughter about her brothers. That smacks of jealousy. Or insecurity. I don't know. I do know that's not how Christians should treat each other."

The mom says nothing, but she turns and glowers at her daughter. A look we've all seen. A look we all know. The daughter squirms.

"Second, I'm very disappointed as a female," I say. "I was really excited about Sydel coming to Charlotte Christian. It was a necessary step for her. She was leaving my school as one of the older students, having been taught, hopefully, how to be a leader herself. And then she comes to this new school excited, motivated, and she is treated this way on her first day? My daughter came in looking up to your daughter. Your daughter had an opportunity to be a leader, a role model. I'm speaking for my daughter right now—which I try not to do—but she felt really hurt."

The other mom shifts uncomfortably. I can tell by her expression that what I'm saying has hit home. I should probably back off now, but I can't help myself. I want to drive home a final point.

"Your daughter forfeited a golden opportunity," I say. "She had a chance to make a positive difference in a younger Black female's life."

I glance around the room and I lower my voice.

"There are very few African American people at that school. Everyone notices us. They watch us. They put us in a sort of spotlight. They see how we treat each other. We should be supporting each other. The *girls* should be supporting each other."

Silence. The other mom fixes her eyes on her daughter, study-ing her, watching her, assessing her. I can see by the expression on the daughter's face that she wishes she could disappear. I glance at Sydel. For a moment, she holds back a smile. Then she, too, looks at the girl and her expression changes. I can feel Sydel's empathy radi-ating. She can sense how hard this conversation must be for the girl.

"I have to tell you," the mom says to me. "I appreciate you coming to me with your daughter and speaking directly to both me and my daughter. We are going to go home now and we are going to talk about this. We have a lot to discuss."

Another glance at her daughter. This time her daughter looks off longingly toward the door.

"I want to thank you," the mom says. "Sydel, I'm confident you will see a change at school."

The mom will not only be accurate, she will be prophetic. Sydel and her daughter will become friends and eventually teammates on the high school volleyball team.

But at the moment, I say, "I want to thank *you* for listening and for understanding. And for being so open."

The mom and daughter leave. Sydel and I watch them go.

"That was—amazing," Sydel says.

"It went well," I say. "But it could've gone the other way. The mom could have gotten upset or defensive or who knows what. You never know how she might have taken it. She could've lashed out. When you confront someone like that, you are taking a chance."

"It was worth it."

"In this case, yes."

"I would be willing to take the chance," Sydel says. "In the future."

"Good. And I believe most people will be respectful of you—if you treat them with respect. That's the key. Have courage—the courage of your convictions—and approach people with respect."

"Like you said, it may not work. What should you do then?"

"If all else fails?"

"Yes."

I pause and then I say, "At that point, as your grandma would say, 'You can commence to whupping some tail.'"

Sydel has reached that age.

Meaning—she has started noticing boys and boys are seriously starting to notice her.

I pray about this. Well, I've been praying and anticipating and worrying about this phase for a while. As a first step, I invite Sydel to join me in a six-week devotion called "Pathways to Duty," which centers on a woman's self-worth as a child of God. Once a week, we spend a day together, reading Scripture and discussing romantic relationships. We always include a field trip. We go to the botanical gardens or a bookstore or to a restaurant for afternoon tea. We settle in, two ladies talking about women and men, what to embrace in a relationship, what to look out for, and what to avoid. One day, as I pour our tea, I say, "It comes down to this. Do you want to be treated like fine china or a Styrofoam cup?"

I fill her teacup, then mine, and then I stir in some sugar.

"Think about it. Styrofoam. You pour in what you're drinking and when you're done, you throw the container away. Or fine china. When you're finished, you clean your cup carefully, you take care of it, you put it in a safe place, you cherish it."

"I want to be treated like fine china," she says. "Always."

"Because that's who you are," I say. "Never forget that."

As Sydel enters high school, her social life threatens to dominate most of her free time. That's how I see her, anyway. My social butterfly. At school, even as a freshman, she becomes a standout volleyball player, a central reason the team surges through the state playoffs and makes it all the way to the semifinals. This success with volleyball conflicts with the start of basketball season. And Dell agrees, Sydel may be an even better basketball player.

She'll just have to juggle both volleyball and basketball for a couple of weeks, I think. It's not that big a deal.

"So, I've made a decision," Sydel tells me one day. "I'm going to quit basketball."

I feel as if she's reared back and kicked me in the gut. I stammer, and then I say, "You—*what?* Why? No. You can do both."

I'm losing it. I sound somewhere between insane and insanely pushy. I pause, breathe, force a smile, quiet my voice.

"Sydel, you have to play basketball. You're so good. It's a family thing. Following in your dad's footsteps. Your brothers—"

"I don't really want to, Mom. It's too much."

"Too much—*what?* What is too much? What?"

"Time, Mom. It takes up too much time. And honestly? I don't really like it that much."

"Since when?"

"A while now. Mom, I want to be with my friends. I'm missing out on stuff."

There you go. There it is.

Missing out on stuff.

Meaning—

Boys.

Missing out on being with boys.

I want to scream all that in her face. I want to shake her, remind her of our six-week devotion, our talks, our intimate conversations, our mommy-daughter tea parties. I have to talk her out of quitting. What argument can I make? Forget that. What can I offer her? Should I bribe her? Someone once told me that the key to parenting is bribery. Who said that? Not me. I wouldn't know how to do that. What would my daughter even want?

Sonya, why are you even thinking this way?

What's the matter with you?

"So, yeah," Sydel says. "I'm not going to play anymore."

I feel my entire body stiffen.

"Call your dad," I say. "Tell him you're not going to play. See what he says."

"Sure. But I've already made up my mind."

Sydel calls Dell. I pace in the other room as she tells her father, NBA player Dell Curry, that she is going to quit basketball, the family sport. He is going to go ballistic.

"Well, babe," Dell says on the phone, "if you don't want to play basketball, that's okay. It's your decision."

Later, when Dell returns from his road trip, we have it out.

"That's not what I wanted you to say. I wanted you to get her to keep playing. She has a talent. She's good. Did you tell her that?"

"You have to calm down."

"I am calm. She could be really good. *Really* good."

"Yes, she's good."

He waits, looks me right in the eye, and says, "But she doesn't want to play. You've got to let it go. You've got to let her be."

Let it go?

No. Not when I know she's making a mistake. She has a

fifteen-year-old mind. She's not thinking right. She's allowing other factors—*boys*—to influence her decision-making. I am going to talk to her. I'll set her straight.

I barge into Sydel's room, prepared to argue her back onto the basketball team, to show her that she's quitting for all the wrong reasons, when something on her wall stops me in my tracks. A saying she's written.

"I am the hero of my own story."

Sydel has written those words in big bold colorful letters.

I stare at that sentence. I think about all the sayings, the lines of Scripture I've written all over the house, plastered on the whiteboard in the kitchen, or written in the kids' rooms. Words, prayers, blessings, quotes that I want them to see and somehow absorb. These words seeping through their skin. From the walls into their heads. Into their hearts. Words to live by. Sydel has done the same thing. She has role-modeled me. I stare at her wall, at that saying, at those words, and my argument against her quitting basketball fritters away, dissolves into dust.

"Mom?"

Her voice sounds far away. I can barely hear her. But then she speaks again and draws me back to reality, to this spot in her room.

"Are you okay?"

"Yeah." I plop down on her bed and look at her, my beautiful social butterfly, sweet, empathetic soul, gifted athlete, and I realize that what I want doesn't matter. I want her to play basketball not for her, but for me. I want to live that sport again, vicariously.

"I came in to talk you into staying with basketball," I say.

"I figured."

"I'm not going to do that. I changed my mind."

I look up at her wall and read that saying again.

I am the hero of my own story.

"I have to let you make your own choices," I say. "Make them and own them."

"I know. That's what you taught me. I'm going to play volleyball and have a social life."

"You can have it all," I say.

"I can. Just not all at the same time."

I laugh.

"Write your own story," I say. "Make yourself the hero."

These days, I find myself walking with the Lord so deeply and so intensely that I sometimes lose myself in a kind of trance. I allow myself this feeling. I give myself over to it and as I do, I feel myself being awakened, opening up to new possibilities. I seem to be drawn not just to new ideas but also to new people. People I've never met come to me, seeking me out, calling me or approaching me for advice, or even just to talk. Something brand new is happening. It feels stunning and strange and miraculous. I know that God is sending these people to me, for me, to help me, even as I help them.

One day after church, our pastor's sister approaches me. She's a dynamic woman, very prominent and present in the church. Three times a year, our church presents an evening devoted to women's issues, usually with a guest speaker. The pastor's sister coordinates these events.

"Sonya," she says to me, her eyes brimming, filled with kindness. "I have watched you. I've watched your family, your children. We see you, your spirit of praise, and we're all moved by it. I was wondering—would you be willing to speak at one of our women's events?"

I am so taken aback and unnerved that for a moment I can't speak.

Why are y'all watching me? I think.

Before I can respond, I actually laugh. I shake my head and I mutter, "Okay, Lord, this is one of Your things, isn't it?"

"Excuse me?" the pastor's sister says.

"I'm sorry," I say. "I'm just so surprised. And flattered. Don't get me wrong. But I think I'll have to say—"

I'm about to say, "No," thinking, *Nope. I can't do this. I'm not speaking in front of fifteen hundred people. Uh-uh. Not me.*

"Don't tell me no now," the pastor's sister says. "Go home and pray about it and we'll talk next week. Let's do it that way, okay?"

"Sure. Okay. That'll work. Thank you for asking me."

She takes my hands. "We'll talk next week."

So I pray about it.

The first thing I admit to God is that I'm scared.

"Lord, I am frightened. Scared to death. Why would she ask me? I'm shaking thinking about it *here*, in the comfort of my home. So, Lord, let me ask You straight up. Are You telling me that I am supposed to do this thing? Is that what You're saying?"

Silence.

The night closes in.

I hear the flutter of a breeze. The rattling of a shade. The hum of air-conditioning.

The silence thickens, darkness enfolds me, and then—clarity.

My verse, I think.

The verse I refer to constantly.

I snap on my nightlight, pick up my Bible, flip it open, go right to it.

Romans 8:28.

I read, "And we know that in all things God works for the good of those who love Him, who have been called according to His purpose."

I read the verse again. I read it *again*, aloud. I read it a third time. This time I practically shout it. And then I read it a fourth time in a whisper.

Then I say, "Do You—do You actually love me enough—love me despite all of my crap before You saved me? You must. You do. Oh, Lord, I have to come to grips with that. It's *hard*."

I sigh, close the Bible, return it to my nightstand, and say, "Okay. It's time, isn't it? It's time to give my testimony."

I don't wait a week.

I call the pastor's sister the next day and tell her I'll do it.

I have thirty days to prepare.

I begin by reading the whole chapter, verse by verse, line by line, word by word. Paul the Apostle authored this chapter in which he discusses our inner struggle between flesh and the spirit. *The story of my life*, I think. And now as Sydel goes through puberty and deals with boys, abandons basketball, and as she will no doubt face her own conflicts of flesh versus spirit, I see that this chapter is the story of her life, too. I have so much to tell her. I've lived through so many experiences, agonized over difficult decisions, made many mistakes. I learned from all this, gained insight, and I believe, some degree of wisdom. Until now, I have been reluctant to share my most difficult and painful experiences with my daughter. That's not true. I haven't been reluctant. I have been afraid.

Given this opportunity to speak at the church, I'm ready to open myself to her. I somehow feel the need to reveal certain secrets that I've kept from her, truths about me that I think she needs to hear because she will benefit from hearing about my humanity, as unflattering and as difficult as these truths may be. It's weird that I feel safer speaking in front of fifteen hundred people than I do speaking directly to her. I wonder why. Safety in numbers? Perhaps. Putting myself at a distance rather than, say, sitting across from her face-to-face? Maybe. I also know that if I commit to this speaking engagement, I can't back down and I can't put off what I want to tell her until some later date. I do want to bond with Sydel, but even more, I desperately want to groom her as a woman. I want her to know my hardest truths.

As I go through Romans, I take notes on every verse. I write in a frenzy. I write personally, intimately, the words pouring out as if channeled through some other source, a reservoir of emotion and experience locked up deep inside me, next to my heart. I imagine speaking these words in front of the packed congregation, and as I do, I know I will be speaking directly to my daughter.

I step up to the lectern in front of the crowd of fifteen hundred worshippers. I clear my throat, smooth out the papers of my speech to steady my nerves. As soon as I start speaking, God comes in, calms me down, lifts my voice, and my nerves settle. I anchor myself by keeping eye contact with Sydel, who sits close to the front. I begin by describing the six weeks we shared doing devotions, visiting various sites around town. Then I ask those assembled before me the same question I asked Sydel: "Do you want to be a Styrofoam cup or refined china?" I explain the meaning and then I add a third option—a plastic cup, something you can use once or twice, but doesn't last beyond that. The congregation laughs, nods, speaks out in confirmation. They get my analogy. I catch Sydel's eye. She nods and laughs, too.

Then I get personal.

I reveal that before I gave birth to Stephen, I had an abortion. I talk about how excruciatingly difficult it was to make that decision, the agony and uncertainty I felt, the anxiety, the loss of sleep. The day of the procedure remains fuzzy, a blur. Maybe I've suppressed most of the details because of how painful it is now to relive that day. My memory hurts. It feels almost unreal, almost as if I'm looking back at another person, not me, or that I'm watching a movie of someone else's life.

As I speak now, I look at Sydel. She watches me intently. I can read her expression: *Mom, wow, too much information, but—I am glad to be hearing this.*

And then—I can almost see her coming of age right before my eyes. I ask God for courage and I ask Him to give my daughter courage to understand that I'm sharing this story for her benefit, to warn her, to help her, and to help anyone else in the congregation who may be facing a similar decision.

"Find the strength to admit you're human," I say. That's why I'm here, speaking in front of all these people. People know me here, in this community. "Like all of you, I'm flawed. I'm real. I'm human."

Then I talk about getting pregnant a year or so after the abortion and deciding against having an abortion a second time. I take the audience on the trip through my life. I tell everyone how hard it was getting married while I was still in college and how much it pained me to leave school before I graduated. I talk about what it feels like being married to an NBA player. Of course, NBA wives receive a lot of perks, but sometimes people view us as appendages. Accoutrements. Even, on occasion, we seem invisible. To illustrate, I tell a story about an incident that occurred a few years into Dell's NBA career.

We'd run out of bread at the house and we popped into a local grocery store. Dell wandered off to browse while I grabbed a loaf of bread. I took my place in the checkout line and placed my loaf of bread on the conveyor in front of the cashier.

"Loaf of wheat bread," he said, tapping his cash register. "That'll be a dollar ninety-nine."

At that moment, he noticed Dell standing behind me.

"Oh, I'm sorry, Mr. Curry, I didn't see you there." The cashier looked back at me. "I apologize, Mrs. Curry. I didn't realize that it was you."

"Yes. I'm his wife. My name is Sonya."

"You go on through."

"What about the bread?"

"No charge. It's on me."

I hold for a moment in front of the congregation, allowing the story to sink in. I hear the audience shifting in their seats, murmuring, responding viscerally to the story.

"Now, I appreciate Sonya *Curry,* the *Curry* part," I say to the congregation. "I truly do. But I want to be *Sonya.* I want you to know that I am here. I *exist.* I am my own person. My own woman. I have my own identity. I want all you women here—women of every age—to be seen and appreciated for who you are—not for who you supposedly *belong to* . . . outside of God."

The congregation reacts, loudly.

"By the way, I paid for that bread."

The congregation erupts. I look at Sydel. She's grinning widely and joining everyone else in applause.

Driving home after giving the speech, Sydel and I sit in silence. I'm pumped up, energized. I need to decompress. I wonder how she feels. I know she hadn't expected me to be so forthcoming, so raw, so revealing.

"You saw a whole new side of me," I say.

"Yeah."

"Are you okay?"

"Yes," she says, then adds, "I am."

"Were you uncomfortable?"

She thinks about this, swivels her head toward me. "Maybe a little. For a minute. It didn't last. I'm okay now."

"As long as you're okay and we're okay."

"We are."

I grip the steering wheel, look straight ahead, try to speak casually. "Do you want to talk about anything?"

"No. I mean—I don't think so. Not now, anyway."

"Okay. I know it was a lot."

"Yeah."

I look at Sydel again and this time I see that she's smiling.

"I'll admit that I was a little nervous about talking in front of all those people," I say.

"It didn't show."

"Well, thanks. The power of prayer. I felt I was in His hands."

I pause then, keeping my eyes focused on the road.

"I want you to know something else. It's important." I take a breath and then I say, "Nobody is perfect. Not me, not your father, not your brothers, nobody. We strive to be the best we can be, but we are imperfect. It took a lot of prayer, strength, faith—a ton of inner work to get to where I am today."

She nods.

I go silent. I think about what I went through, the path I took to get here. The road I traveled that allowed me to speak in front of the congregation, and to believe—to know—that I had something to say, values, a life experience to share. In order to get here, though, I needed to clean up my stuff. All of it. I couldn't move on with my life until I did all that. I feel thankful that God chose me, despite all that. I didn't offer up myself, saying, *God, please take me because I'm this great person.* I was aware of all my baggage. My imperfections. And still God saved me. Now I'm acutely aware of my imperfections. I live with them, and I no longer feel stuck. I feel healed. Tonight, by revealing myself publicly and especially to my daughter, I feel that I have not only dealt with certain issues by speaking them aloud, I have released their grip on me. Something profound has changed within me. It feels as if I have come to a turning point in my life, and in my parenting.

"Sydel, you've seen me in action when there's an issue. You've observed me. I'm the person people come to, at school, at home, to be the problem solver. Everybody seems to think that I have the answers, the solutions. Well, I do what I can, but I make mistakes. You will, too. I wanted to take the pressure off you by showing you what I went through. You'll have your own stuff. We know that. Maybe you won't go through the same stuff I did. I was alone. I was scared. Maybe by speaking tonight, I struck a chord, helped somebody."

Sydel turns to me. "You were good, Mom. Everybody loved it."

I glance at her and I see something in her eyes, an emotion that causes me to tear up.

I see pride. A daughter's pride.

"I want you to know something else. Your value—your worth—has nothing to do with what you have. You can have everything in the world. Every material possession you could want. Those things don't matter. Because inside, you may be struggling. You may have a void. Your worth is what God thinks you are. Who God says you are. Do you understand that?"

"I do."

"You know what I want for you?" I ask.

"What?"

"I want you to live the saying you put up on your wall. I want you to be the hero of your own story."

20

I'll Take Him Just the Way He Is

STEPHEN HAS nearly completed his junior year of college. Seth will soon be finishing his freshman year. Sydel will begin high school in the fall.

Where did the time go?

Spring 2009.

Bathed by moonlight, I kneel on the floor of Stephen's empty room, close my eyes, and pray.

"Lord, please, let him do the right thing."

In a few hours, Stephen will take a seat in front of members of the media, and facing a swirl of cameras and microphones, he will announce his decision to the world, to his teammates, his coach, his friends, and his family. He will tell us his future. Nobody knows what he will say. Nobody knows the decision he will announce. Nobody. Including me.

I am nervous about his decision.

That's not true. That doesn't come close to expressing how I feel. I'm an emotional wreck. I'm filled with worry, doubt, fear, and anxiety. I have tried to calm myself and settle my nerves by praying for him, praying hard and often. I whisper my prayers, recite them silently, say them aloud. As usual, I don't only speak them. I write my prayers down on slips of paper and in my journals.

"Lord," I say, "I'm praying for Stephen. I've got to trust You with him. God, please give him wisdom, give him clarity, give him sound judgment in making this decision. I've done my best to prepare him in life. I now turn him over to You. I pray that he has learned to seek Your guidance."

Now . . . when you hear what I'm praying for, you may very well think, What? *Is she serious? Why do you need to pray to God for that?*

I'm sure most folks may call what we're facing a first-world problem, a win-win situation. Stephen, one of the best college basketball players in the country, the nation's top scorer, averaging 28.6 points a game, consensus First Team All-American, Southern Conference Player of the Year, is about to announce whether he's leaving Davidson College after his junior year to declare for the NBA draft. Why is this even a problem? Why is Stephen—and why am I—agonizing over this decision?

Well, to begin with, this has nothing to do with basketball.

This is all about keeping a promise. Honoring a commitment. As we say in Montessori, *completion of task*. Stephen's decision takes me back to my own decision to leave college when I was a junior to join Dell and to give birth to Stephen. But eventually, I went back to college and completed my task. I earned my degree. Stephen has assured me and his coach, Bob McKillop, that he will get his degree.

He told me that I would watch him walk in his cap and gown at his graduation and receive his college diploma.

But what's the big deal? Why should I care if he leaves college after his junior year? Many basketball players leave college after their *freshman* year.

Not Stephen. That's not how I raised him. That's not who he is. He doesn't leave anything unfinished. He sees everything through to the end. He does his work; he completes his task. He never, *ever* quits. Leaving college before he finishes would be totally out of character.

I know. I have to back off. This is his choice, his future, not mine. His life, not mine.

Still—

That night, the moonlight trickling onto the floor of Stephen's empty room, I finish my prayer, get up off my knees, and wander through our house, feeling unsteady and anxious. As I walk, I murmur, "Why do I feel this way? This should be a time of *joy*. Why do I feel so—anxious?"

No matter how much I pray, no answer comes.

The next morning, Dell and I go to Stephen's press conference at Davidson, only a half-hour drive from our home. I arrive at the gym, a nervous wreck, still not knowing what Stephen will say, as much in the dark as anyone else. I'm not surprised that Stephen has not yet told us his decision. He may not even know himself. He has so much information and emotion to weigh. All the experts and NBA insiders we've talked to have said that if Stephen declares for the draft now, he will certainly go in the first ten picks. That would be a sound, smart decision. He's certainly NBA ready.

Why play his senior year and risk injury? Or maybe he'll be distracted or feel undue pressure to excel and have a down year and his stock may fall. Being an optimist, and his mother, I counter that argument with, "He'll be stronger, more savvy, more motivated, and I believe he'll have a *better* year." And in that case, he'll complete college, graduate, and when he gets drafted next year, he'll not only go in the top ten picks, he could go number one.

Dell and I take our positions to the side of the scrum of media that's forming in the Davidson gym. My thoughts waver. First, I think, *Oh, he's absolutely going to stay for his senior year,* then a second later, I think, *He's definitely going to declare for the draft.*

Finally, Stephen appears. He moves in front of the cameras. Stephen makes eye contact with us, nods, then looks over at Coach McKillop, who's standing to the side. He grins at his coach, shooting him that contagious, boyish smile. I study my son's face and then suddenly he morphs into a little kid, my eight-year-old Stephen—sweet, generous, the peacemaker who wants to solve every problem rapidly and in the fairest way, always inclusive and fair, and then his face broadens and—blip—he returns to his full, adult form. He leans into the microphone in front of him and says, "I've decided to declare—"

I don't hear the rest.

Dell begins to applaud, then turns and beams at me, his wide smile full of joy and pride.

I don't applaud. I can't. I force a smile back.

But I feel numb.

The short press conference ends, and members of the media, friends, and family crowd around Stephen. I knife my way through the mass of people and arrive next to him. He says, "Mom," and

I say, "Oh, Steph, I'm so proud," and then I hug him with all my might, but I turn my head so he can't see the tears sliding down my cheeks.

He pulls away, gently, swallowed by his teammates, and I feel myself gasp.

"Sonya," Dell says, reaching for me.

"I'm okay," I say, and then I say, "I'm going to go."

"Where?"

"I don't know."

I turn and walk out of the building.

I go to a movie called *August Rush.* I get lost in the story of an eleven-year-old musical prodigy who has been separated from his mother and lives in an orphanage. He runs away to New York City while his mother, believing he's alive, desperately searches for him. When he finally reunites with his mother, I sit alone in the dark of the theater and sob.

I think of three years earlier.

Stephen, a senior in high school, sat in our living room, slightly nervous, but mainly confident, his fingers laced in front of him. He bounced to the edge of his chair. Dell and I sat on the couch across from Bob McKillop, the basketball coach at Davidson College. We have all convened here on the occasion of Stephen coming to another decision, whether or not he should go to Davidson and play for Coach McKillop.

It's funny, I think now, sitting in the dark of the movie theater. *Today, I don't want him to leave Davidson. Three years ago, I didn't want him to go.*

Despite his success in high school, few Division I schools recruited Stephen. Those coaches saw a skinny kid who looked like he'd be pushed around. Of course, they didn't know Stephen. They didn't know about his toughness, his determination, his work ethic. Then Coach McKillop saw Stephen play and came after him, hard. I wasn't convinced. I needed to be persuaded. I felt that Davidson was too close. I wanted Stephen to go to a school that was farther away, not thirty minutes down the road. I wanted him to experience college life away from us. I believed that would help him mature.

At first, when Stephen mentioned Davidson, I dismissed the idea. For a month, Stephen asked me to watch him play at open gym and meet Coach McKillop. I flat out refused. Stephen wouldn't give up. He said, "Mom, please, Davidson is two exits away from your school. Come over at lunch. Come for an hour."

"If I do, will you stop asking me?"

"Yes," he said.

As a courtesy to Stephen, I went one lunchtime to see him play. One hour, that's all I promised. That's all it took. I loved how Coach McKillop related to both the players on the team and the ones coming in. I loved his confidence, how he carried himself. Most of all, I saw how Stephen responded to him. I saw how happy he seemed. I fell in love with Davidson. I bought in, all the way.

Then Coach McKillop came to our house. He stayed for quite some time, but Stephen, Dell, and I made our decision in the first two minutes.

"I know how you raise your children," Coach McKillop said to us. "I know how important the spiritual aspect is to you—and to Stephen. I will do more than encourage that. I will honor that."

We asked him a few more questions, and then Stephen said, "Mom, I want to sign with him."

We agreed. Stephen would go to Davidson. I walked Coach McKillop to the door and I said, "Thank you, Coach. And I promise I will fatten him up for you."

Coach McKillop rested his hands on my shoulders and looked me in the eye.

"Sonya," he said. "I will take him just the way he is."

I relive that moment in the movie theater and the tears come again. Finally, as the credits roll, I realize that I've cried myself out.

"Have your moment," I tell myself, thinking about Stephen and the decision he's just made. "Because from now on, you have to show him nothing but love and support. Let go and let God."

I do—always.

But I cry because I feel loss.

Deep, gut-wrenching loss.

I didn't want him to go to a school so close to home. But today, after he's declared for the NBA, I am not ready for him to leave.

This isn't about Stephen, my firstborn, my sensitive son, the child I always felt the need to protect, the little boy and then the young man who would always try to please, to do the right thing. He is moving on. He is moving away. I cried when Stephen made his announcement because *I* am not ready.

I live my life trying to plan ahead, always trying to prepare. If I can impart one lesson, it's that one word: *prepare*.

But no matter how much you prepare, you will always be blindsided. Life constantly throws you curveballs. How you deal with those will pretty much determine the quality of your life.

In that movie theater, feeling loss and feeling lost, I whisper a question to God.

"Lord," I say, "what is my purpose now?"

Oh, Sonya, there will always be a purpose. You just have to find it.

Stephen has made his decision. He has made it and he has owned it. He has his purpose.

Stephen leaves Davidson after his junior year.

The Golden State Warriors pick him seventh in the 2009 NBA Draft.

21

Respect

APRIL 2008.

Under the radar.

That's where Seth, a high school senior, has flown.

Surprising since he led his high school, Charlotte Christian, to an appearance in the state finals and finished senior year averaging 22.3 points, 5 assists, and 5 rebounds per game. He's been named All-Conference, All-State, and what makes me proudest—First Team Scholastic All-American. And yet, most Division I schools ignored him. I believe he blames me for making him miss that tournament. In my opinion, the D-I coaches simply missed him. They didn't see him. As we say, he didn't pass their "eye test."

"Respect," he murmurs, in this case meaning the *lack of.*

So many times, I have called him out for mumbling. Normally, I would say, "What? I can't hear you" to try to get him to speak louder—*respectfully*—but this time, as we drive to his high school where he will officially sign up to attend Liberty University, I don't bother. I know what he means. I know what my son longs for. Just that. Respect. It's what I want for him, too.

Respect has become his key word. What drives him and what defines him. What he wants and deserves—what he believes everyone wants and deserves.

"If you earn it," I say.

In terms of basketball and scholastics, Seth has earned respect. Nobody can deny that.

I think of a Scripture from Romans 13:7.

"Pay to all what is owed . . . respect to whom respect is owed, honor to whom honor is owed."

And still, not a sniff of interest from Duke, or Kentucky, or Kansas, or any of the top Division I schools. Why? I don't know, but at one point, I think I hear someone mutter a half-baked explanation, "He's a shooting guard in a point guard's body."

So, here we are, pulling into the parking lot for Signing Day. Dell finds a space, and he, Seth, and I slowly, almost hesitantly, emerge from the car. We head toward the gym, Seth's home away from home, where his high school will host what has become a tradition—the annual celebration of the seniors who will go on to play sports at the various colleges they will attend. Seth has chosen Liberty for several reasons, including, of course, its basketball program, led by Coach Ritchie McKay. Coach McKay has sold us on the school, emphasizing its strong educational environment, spiritual shepherding, and his desire to coach Seth. We are well aware of Liberty, an evangelical school founded by Jerry Falwell Jr. It all seems so—perfect.

Too perfect.

As we start to walk into the gym, a sudden wave of nausea courses through my stomach and rises into my throat.

Oh no, I think. *Not now.*

My stomach flips, I sigh and say to myself, *Yep. It's happening.* I place my hands over my midsection. I can almost trace the gyration. I sigh again, deeper, attempting to settle myself. I know what this is—the rolling in my gut and soul that overtakes me when God is about to reveal something. I know this feeling well. I can't call it a common feeling, but it's certainly familiar. This gyration rumbles through my stomach either when something feels off or something unexpected, out of the blue, is about to happen. A warning. I never know when that unknown *something* will occur or what it will be. I just have to gear myself up because I know at some point, it will happen. It's happened too many times.

I experience these feelings most often at night, in bed. The gyrating sensation in my stomach will jar me awake. I know by now that it's God getting in touch. Grabbing my attention. He will literally jolt me out of sleep. Of course, He doesn't tell me why. He just announces, loud and clear, *Sonya, something's coming. Get ready.*

I suppose you can call these prophetic dreams, or visions, or premonitions. Whatever you want to call them, I know they are real. By now, I don't exactly expect them, but I'm not surprised by them. I'm prepared to deal with them.

At night, when I faith walk with God after He wakes me with a jolt to the gut, I talk to Him directly.

"Father," I say. "I get it. I hear You. I *feel* You. But You need to tell me what to do. You brought me here. You brought this feeling to me. You've got to get me through this. Please."

Now, on this warm April day in 2008—Signing Day at Charlotte Christian—I receive the gyration in my stomach with Seth on one side, Dell on the other. Seth sees the look on my face and eyes me with concern, and then he sighs with resignation. He knows about my feelings. My premonitions. He'll shrug and mutter, "Nothing I can do about it."

Dell waits. He knows I am about to drop some kind of bomb on him. He shifts his weight, preparing himself for whatever it is I'm about to tell him. He's getting ready to take action or duck for cover.

I pull Dell aside and I whisper, "It's happening. I'm getting that feeling."

"What? *Now?*"

"Dell, I don't know if Seth is supposed to sign right now."

Coach Brown appears and slides past us. He glances at his watch. "We're almost ready to start. I'll see you inside."

He pats Seth on the back, grins, and heads into the gym.

We look at Seth. He looks beyond confused.

"Go inside," I say to him. "We'll be right in."

He shakes his head. I wait for him to disappear inside the gym. I face Dell. "I have to figure this out."

Dell looks completely baffled.

"I'm going to call my cousin," I say.

My cousin, a coach who knows the coaching business and the people in it, has been an invaluable source of information and guidance during this process with Seth. I call him, frantically.

"Hi. I know this is going to sound weird—"

He doesn't let me finish. He cracks up. He knows me. We grew up together. "What is it, girl?"

"We are here, right now, at Charlotte Christian. Seth has gone into the gym to *sign*. It's Signing Day."

"Okay, calm down. Take a deep breath. Now, let's talk this through."

"One last time. I promise."

"As many times as you need," my cousin says.

We talk about Liberty University, Coach McKay, the basketball program, and our spiritual expectations. Finally, my cousin says, "So add that all up. What do you have? Meaning, are you sure this is where Seth should go?"

"Not really. I don't know."

"He's going to be there for four years."

"I'm so frantic." I take a deep breath and close my eyes. "I feel—"

I squeeze my eyes tighter. "I feel that this is the right decision— for now, for right now, for today, but this may not be the end."

I open my eyes. "That's all I can see. That's all I know to say. I can't explain any more to you."

My cousin laughs again. "Sonya, I get it. Seth will be all right. You'll be all right, too."

I thank him and hang up as Dell and Seth walk toward me. Now they both look confused.

"What's going on?" Seth says.

"I had to check on something," I say. "I'll be honest with you. I'm not one hundred percent sure about this choice."

I look at Seth, at Dell, then I look back at my son. Poor Seth. He doesn't know where to look.

"I got the okay from God that we can walk forward in this decision," I say. "But I am telling you that we will be revisiting this choice at some point."

"Okay, Mom," Seth says, resigned, ready to move on. "So can I sign?"

I nod. "We are coming in with you. We're with you."

He heads back into the gym. Dell and I hang back a step or two behind our son. As we walk into the gym, I catch Dell shaking his head, muttering, "My wife."

Seth spends a tumultuous freshman year at Liberty. He plays his heart out, but he doesn't love the school or the environment. "It's not my flavor," he says. On the basketball team, he occasionally sulks, zones out, doesn't pay attention. He protects himself by disappearing inside himself. He acts out in small ways; arriving late at practice is his default and most defiant move. He pays the price for that as the coach doesn't start him the next game. As the year goes on, it becomes clear to Dell and me that Seth doesn't belong at Liberty academically, socially, or on the basketball court. I become adamant about it, even desperate. One day, I blurt to Dell, "We have to make a change." In spite of everything, remarkably, Seth finds his way. He is the ultimate "next play" person. He will not allow himself to become stuck in junk. He rises to every occasion, plays every hand he's dealt to the fullest. I admire that so much. I admire *him*. Even though he doesn't really fit at Liberty, Seth finishes the season leading the country's freshmen in scoring, averaging 20.2 points per game.

In 2009, I fly to California to watch Stephen play in the National Invitation Tournament. Davidson will be playing St. Mary's in what could be Stephen's last college game. With pressure building to find Seth a place to transfer, Dell stays home.

"What are you going to do?" I ask him.

"I don't know. Make some calls. See if I hear anything. You have to be careful."

"I know. It's delicate. I do know we have to make a change."

Sitting in the stands at the St. Mary's college gym in Moraga, California—annoyed that this is a home game for them while Davidson has had to travel nearly three thousand miles—my cell phone bleats a minute before tip-off.

Dell.

"What's going on?"

"Seth's game just ended," he says. "I went into the coach's office and told him Seth's not returning."

I leap to my feet. My heart starts racing.

"Oh. My. *Gosh*," I say.

"Yeah," Dell says. "It's done. He's out."

"How did . . . what did . . . is Seth—?"

The crowd roars. Someone behind me asks me to sit down. I mouth, *Sorry*, and crash-land back on my seat.

"The game just started," I say to Dell.

"It'll be all right," he says. "Cheer on Stephen."

I exhale and actually fan myself with my fingers, feeling as if I might hyperventilate. I click off my phone, put it away, clap my hands, and focus on Stephen.

The game ends. Davidson loses. Stephen's college career comes to a close.

I stand and applaud as the teams leave the basketball court.

My two sons, I think.

One leaving college, going on to the NBA; the other leaving college, going on to—a better place.

Each starting a new journey.

Have faith. Listen. Believe.

I can almost hear His voice speaking to me as if I'm on a midnight prayer walk—

I got you.

Remember, Sonya, I think, reminding myself, *this is what you saw, what you felt, what you dreamed. You envisioned this. You even told Seth that he might be leaving Liberty.* You saw all this. *You're just living it now.*

Then—a challenge.

Every day, for an hour, the entire Liberty University student body—fifteen thousand students—convenes in a large arena for chapel.

The day after Dell meets with Coach McKay to tell him that Seth will be withdrawing from school, the students stream across campus and enter the arena for their daily prayer. By now, word has spread. Everyone knows that Seth Curry, one of the top players on the basketball team, the country's leading freshman scorer, will not be returning to school in the fall. This day, Seth, running late for daily prayer, lowers his head and walks into the arena. As he comes in, a buzz starts. An undercurrent. Then the buzz builds into a low, persistent, angry hum. The sound peaks and overflows and the students begin to boo. Fifteen thousand students, sitting in prayer, boo my son.

When he tells me this later, I shudder and I want to shout, but then I think, *You're strong, Seth. You can take it.* Then, counterintuitively, as a form of defense, I laugh.

A second thought follows.

They'll regret booing you. They will. You'll make them regret it.

I have a final thought.

We did the right thing.

Within a week, the calls start coming in. Kentucky. Louisville. North Carolina. And Duke. Coach Mike Krzyzewski wants to meet Seth, Dell, and me. I can't say that I absolutely know, without a doubt, that Seth should go to Duke, but I feel myself leaning in that direction, by reputation alone. First, I thank God for giving Seth this opportunity. I want to pinch myself. I do know that Coach K is exactly what Seth needs—a hard-nosed disciplinarian, the coach who prepares all his players for the next stage, the NBA. Sitting across from Coach K in his office, I realize that we can't really impress him. He knows who he is and what he expects from his players.

"Well, I have a few questions," I say at one point, and then I shrug, "I mean, I can't *not* ask you a few questions."

Coach K laughs. "I've heard about you, Sonya."

We all laugh, Seth maybe the loudest.

Coach K leans forward. "Okay, I'm ready."

I bring up the importance of spirituality in our lives and in our family. I look at Seth and I feel the emotion rise into my throat. We sit quietly for a moment. Seth folds his hands and stares at them.

Coach K breaks the silence, "I know how important religion is to you and to your family. If this works out, Seth will find a very comfortable spiritual environment at Duke, if that's what he chooses. It'll be up to him. I will keep an eye on him, as I do on all my players. I can promise you that."

Seth and Dell nod, seemingly in unison. I clasp my hands and say, "Well, I have another question."

Coach K grins. "Okay."

"What about the mascot?"

"The—mascot?"

"Yeah. The Duke Blue Devil. Speaking of our religious concerns, my child is not playing for no *devil*."

Coach K loses it. We all crack up, including Dell and Seth, who both look mortified.

"All right," Coach K says, still chuckling. "Let me explain where that mascot comes from. It's a devil ray. A fish."

"So it's not religious."

"Not at all."

"In that case, to avoid confusion, maybe you should change it."

Two days before Seth's deadline to sign, we tour Duke again, but I think we've all made our decision before we get out of the car. As a transfer student, Seth will have to sit out a year before he can play on the basketball team. We all feel it's worth it. We choose Duke and Coach K.

Seth does fairly well his sophomore season and even better his junior season. Toward the end of his junior year, Coach K sits down with Seth for a heart-to-heart.

"Seth, I have no doubt you could be an NBA player, but frankly, you're not giving it your best shot. To be blunt, you have to give more effort. A lot more effort."

I'd had that exact conversation with Seth, almost word for word. Mine went nowhere. Maybe he'd listen to Coach K.

He does. Seth turns it on senior year. He starts every game, averages 17.5 points per game and is named to the All-Atlantic Coast Conference First Team and Second Team All-America. He achieves this without practicing. What people don't know is that he plays with a stress fracture in his right leg. Coach K and the team doctor allow Seth to play, as long as he alleviates some of the pressure on his leg by not practicing. He graduates from Duke, but word leaks about his injury and despite his stellar career, he goes undrafted. Seth then begins a torturous and circuitous journey through the NBA, beginning with a short stint on the Golden State Warriors. Over the next six years, he makes several stopovers in the NBA Developmental League, going back and forth from the D-League to the NBA, from Cleveland to Orlando, to Phoenix, to Sacramento. Along the way, he endures two severe leg injuries, eventually putting every ounce of effort he can muster into rehab, always keeping a laser focus on returning to the NBA. He never gives up. He becomes a quiet warrior, always living for the next play. He plays for Dallas, then Sacramento, and ultimately lands in Portland, where he plays a major role on the 2018–19 team that makes a deep run into the playoffs. In that series, Seth and Stephen face each other, going head-to-head, guarding each other, the first time in NBA history two brothers play against each other in the NBA Conference Finals.

I attend every game, laser focused on my sons on the court, cheering for both, trying to be impartial, wearing a Portland jersey for one half, switching to a Golden State jersey at halftime. While drowning in a mother's pride, I agonize over having to split my focus. Seth plays great, but Golden State wins the series 4–0.

Someone—maybe a reporter—asks me how I felt watching my two sons play each other.

"Honestly?" I say. "I was a mess. I'm glad it's over. I'm glad it was quick."

22

Moving Day

I BLINK—and it's gone.

The life I knew.

I wander through the house, alone, imagining their voices, hearing their voices, the voices of my children echoing off the walls—their loud, animated conversation, shouting, arguing, and their laughter. Mostly their laughter. Then beyond their voices, I see images, vivid pictures in my mind—all of us reading Bible devotions at dawn, holding hands across the kitchen table, clustered at the same table for our weekly family meetings, shuttling back and forth to games, cheering on our children, people flowing in and out of the house for our cookouts, and car rides, countless car rides, quiet on the way in, sometimes the kids catching up on sleep, louder on the way back, music playing, and sometimes just quiet, most of us talked out. Again, I hear the laughter. Always laughter. I gravitate toward that. That's what makes my ears perk up, the sound my mind clings to—the laughter. High-pitched, loud, breathless, sometimes hysterical, out-of-control joy.

Oh, how we laughed.

And now, the last in line, Sydel—my baby, my daughter, my buddy—has sent off her final college application. She has completed the paperwork that will result in her going away and my dreaded empty nest. I try not to dwell on it. I try not even to think about it. I can't help it. The idea of the emptiness chokes me. What will I do without her? Now, seven or eight months before she will move on, I cruise the hallway outside her room. I stop, hesitate, and then I pop in, late at night, while she sleeps and watch her, and again, I touch her foot, caress her head. When she's not there, I sit on her floor and stare at her crisply made bed and feel myself consumed by the emptiness in her room. It seeps into my heart. I scan her walls, stare at the photos of her in her volleyball uniform, with a group of friends, with her brothers, and I ask myself, *Where did this striking young woman come from? Who is she? Where did my baby girl go?*

She has inherited the family's athleticism. As her brothers excelled in basketball at Charlotte Christian, Sydel, a lean, strong, five nine, has excelled in volleyball, not only at her school, but also on travel teams all across the state. A four-year starter since freshman year, captain of the high school team from sophomore through senior year, she has led Charlotte Christian to two Division Championships. The offers from colleges come in steadily, as they did with Stephen and Seth, even though the top Division I colleges initially ignored them. Once again, I read Scripture. I pray, asking for guidance. I say aloud, "Father, close the doors You don't want her to go through. And the one left over, we will know without a shadow of a doubt that's where You want her to go."

Strangely, that's how it happens. A tantalizing offer will appear and then for some reason the college will take it off the table.

Perfect. That makes it so much easier.

When she's not looking—as I did with her brothers—I'll scribble a Scripture on a scrap of paper and slip it under her mattress or write a Scripture in big bold colorful letters on her bedroom wall or on the whiteboard in the kitchen. Eventually, Sydel chooses Elon University, a small private university two hours away from home. Close enough so I can attend her volleyball games, far enough for her to feel her independence. As time ticks down and Sydel gets closer to leaving, I offer her this from Matthew 6:33: "Seek you first the kingdom of God and His righteousness, and all things will be added unto you."

Put God first and everything else will follow.

Remember—He only wants what's good for us.

Sydel's senior year of high school ends. We hold the graduation party to end all graduation parties—celebrating her, sending her off into the next phase of her life with a packed house of family and friends, presenting a video of her life that I've compiled, music playing throughout, people offering testimonials and toasts. Ending my dry period of fourteen years, I toast my daughter with a glass of wine. My glass raised, my emotions swelling, I admit that I am having a hard time accepting that my last child will be leaving. My life will be changing. I believe I deserve a drink. I think of Noah returning to shore after the Great Flood, having spent forty days and forty nights in an ark packed tight with all those animals. One of the first things he did on dry land was drink some wine. I can relate. I wouldn't say that we've come out of a once-in-a-lifetime flood, but I feel as if I have washed up on some foreign shore. I'm staring at something new, different. A new land. A new beginning. The voice of God echoes in my head. I start to feel that rumbling in my stomach. Or maybe it's the result of finally having a drink after such a long abstinence, but I hear, loud and clear—*Something's coming, Sonya. Be ready.*

As each day comes and goes, I start to feel increasingly antsy, unmoored. I walk through my life in a daze. When I think about Sydel leaving, a wave of sadness rushes over me. I feel inert. I don't really want to do anything. Sometimes I don't even want to move.

I'm in a slump, I think. *Or maybe I'm having a midlife crisis.*

As I help Sydel pack for school, I not only think about where she's going, her exciting new chapter, I begin reevaluating my own direction. Where am *I* going? Where do I want to be? What do I want to do? What is my purpose now? My daughter is about to head into new territory, facing an exciting, yet somewhat frightening unknown. I start to feel the same way about myself. I've spent five years with her—the two of us—traveling together to volleyball tournaments, sharing hours in the car, bonding sometimes by revealing our deepest thoughts, worries, issues, surprising each other by our honesty, our intimacy. Often, we felt so comfortable together we simply enjoyed sharing the same space, basking in the silence.

Then moving day arrives. I've been anticipating this day, eyeing this day on the calendar, expecting this day, dreading this day. And yet when it arrives, it sneaks up on me. I'm not ready. Sydel is leaving. We have to go. It's time. The end. The beginning.

I help Sydel close her suitcase. I zip it up, and I gasp. I don't think she hears my breathing accelerate because she has turned away. She's studying her walls, her room, taking this moment to say goodbye. I lock onto her intensity with my own feeling of intensity, mirroring hers. Then I feel a pang of finality. Loss. She's going. She's leaving. I am losing my best friend. I feel wrecked. Devastated. Wordlessly, we walk out of her room together. I feel somehow *less*, as if a part of me has been torn off.

Dell drives. I ride shotgun. Sydel spreads herself and her stuff all over the back seat. We don't say much on the two hours or so from our front door to Sydel's dorm, but I lose myself in her excitement. She's brimming with anticipation and eagerness. I go with that. I feel gutted, but I don't let my sadness show. We drive onto campus and I become as captivated and as excited as she is. Elon University feels homey, compact, comfortable, and utterly beautiful, the campus green and blooming as a garden. *This feels like Sydel's place*, I think.

We move her into her room. She chooses her bed, stakes out her half of the room. I help her unpack and we make a list of all the items she needs that we missed—a printer, extra towels, bath sheets. We make a run to the local Bed, Bath & Beyond and then to Best Buy, the same as every incoming freshman at every college across the land. We return, Dell slinging bulging shopping bags over his shoulder. We meet Sydel's roommate and then I help Sydel make her bed and we finish setting up her room. I take my time. I don't want to rush even though I sense how eager Sydel feels to jump into college life. Finally, I can't even pretend that we have more to do. She has moved in and we have to move on. Dell hugs Sydel and leaves me alone with her to say goodbye. We mutter a few mundane final words, clichés that feel hollow. Finally, I straighten up, struggling to hold myself together even as I feel myself falling apart.

Don't cry, I tell myself. *Don't cry in front of her. Be strong, Sonya. Hold yourself together.*

We hug. I choke up as I rub her back. We promise to call, to text, to check in as often as possible but I know it will never be as often as I need. I tell her that I'll go to as many of her volleyball games as I can. We'll see each other often, possibly even weekly.

Then, somehow, I find myself sitting in the car, in the passenger seat, squinting out the window, zoning out as Dell drives home, my thoughts so far away that I'm not even sure where I am. I can't speak. I feel beyond numb. I feel frozen. I try to envision Sydel's future—at least her immediate future. Her volleyball schedule. Classes. Walking across campus. Eating in the dining hall. Studying in her room, in the library. I imagine times that I'll see her. I project weekends. Homecoming. Thanksgiving.

As I picture her future, I think about my own. I see myself walking into my school, losing myself in work, distracting myself, and I wonder—how long do I want to keep doing that? That almost seems behind me now. I have come to a different place, emotionally. I've reached a crossroads. My kids have all entered new stages of their lives. They have all moved on. This feels momentous to me. Life changing. Beyond midlife. I've arrived at a flashing signal indicating that I, too, need a new start.

I think of Sydel and our relationship. I revisit some of the ups and downs we went through. I see her as that fiery five-year-old who tore up her room. I relive her elementary and middle school years—the bullying, her dealing with that and coming out stronger. I remember how I felt when she announced she was quitting basketball. I see the arguments—fights—we had over dating, boys. I feel her sensitivity. Her anxiety. I feel how the two of us battled—sometimes each other—but mostly together, side by side. *She is prepared*, I think. *She will do well.*

I laugh. "Sonya, I hope you do as well."

I never expected that Sydel and I would become so close. We are so deeply, unconditionally connected. I can't count the times I said to my kids together and separately, in frustration, or even in anger, "I am not your friend. I am your *parent*."

Except I was wrong.

Sydel became my closest friend.

As Dell and I drive farther and farther away from her, I feel nothing but loss, and I break down. I cry as if a part of me has died. I cry the rest of the way home. I sob the entire next day and the day after that. And then, like a rainbow appearing after a thunderstorm, my grief lifts, replaced by a low-level melancholy that comes on intermittently, most often when I walk by Sydel's vacant room or after work when I get into my empty car to drive home.

That's when I envision that red blinking light that signals my imaginary—and very real—crossroads.

I have to make changes. Because change is coming.

23

No More Septembers

THE FEELING comes in dreams, during prayers, or snakes into my gut in real time, clenching me, unsettling me. Call it intuition. Call it a sixth sense. I suddenly feel a shift in people's moods, especially those closest to me. I have always been observant, keenly aware of my surroundings, and in tune with people's feelings. This is more than that. This is a physical feeling. I tune in to other people's feelings, especially when something is off, or an attitude has changed. I sense it, I see it, and I want to react.

I will usually want to jump. I think, *Okay, something's off. Let's get at it right now and figure out what's going on. Let's talk it through and then knock it out.*

I want to attack the problem. Hit it head-on. I'm made that way. I'm a fighter. I don't believe that problems go away by themselves. You have to head them off, deal with them. I don't want a problem to fester. I do assess every situation because I may need more information, more evidence, or I may want to observe how a problem will play out before I jump in. But I will never back off from a problem, especially when it involves my kids. I will never allow anyone to hurt them.

Freshman year.

Sydel has a problem.

I sense it.

Something's wrong.

She has a boyfriend and my intuition—my sixth sense—goes haywire.

I don't like this guy. Something about him bothers me. I can't put my finger on what *it* is exactly. It goes beyond a feeling. I see it, I feel it, I sense a shift in energy, beginning with I don't like the way he acts toward Sydel. I definitely see that she's not herself around him. She's off. Way off. She seems gloomy, as if she's carrying a weight. She tries to appear happy, engaged, but it seems forced. I look at her and I can almost see sadness surrounding her. She wears it like a dark gray cloak. I know how that feels. I have only recently shrugged off my heavy coat of sadness. Sydel and I don't really have an opportunity to talk, and I don't want to insert myself into her life without knowing any hard facts, so I don't say anything to her directly. But when I leave after a weekend visiting her, I know without a doubt that something is off.

When I get home, I call two of her volleyball teammates and very close friends.

"This is a very difficult call to make," I say to them. "I realize I'm putting you both on the spot. I hesitate to do that. I do not like to mess in my children's business. And I do not want to compromise your relationship with my daughter in any way, but while this is a very delicate situation, I also believe it's important I talk to you. So I have to ask—is everything okay between her and this boy? I need the truth."

The phone goes quiet. One of the girls clears her throat. Then one of them takes a breath and both of them start speaking urgently, gushing information, talking over each other.

They tell me that they have witnessed Sydel's boyfriend being verbally abusive.

"That's all I need to hear," I say.

I don't need more evidence. I don't require more time. I won't allow this to play out for one more minute. I don't believe Sydel has enough time to sort this out herself. She may soon summon the courage to deal with the boy herself, but I don't know that for sure and I can't take that chance. She's in danger and I need to act. I need to fight. I need to fight for my daughter. I call her immediately.

She sounds relieved and thankful to speak with me, almost as if she has been waiting for my call.

As soon as I mention the boyfriend, she starts crying. Between sobs, she tells me that she doesn't know how to deal with him. She's afraid of how he will react. I ask her if she wants me to intervene.

"Please, Mom," she says. Her voice sounds tiny and distant. In a halting voice between sobs, she gives me his number.

Before I call him, I search my memory. I realize why his name sounds familiar. I know his family from church.

Breathing to calm myself, doing my best to keep my anger from boiling over, I call the boy. He answers. I don't have to introduce myself. He knows who I am.

"I'm calling about you and Sydel," I say.

He instantly gets defensive. "What about us?"

Oh, you have a mouth on you, I think. *Calm yourself, Sonya. Don't lose it.*

"I want to be very respectful right now," I say. "I'm going to be careful with my words. Words matter."

I pause because I want him to hear that. I want him to hear that so much that I repeat the sentence.

"*Words matter.* Now, I realize you are someone else's child so I want you to know that out of respect to you and your parents, I will be calling them right after this phone call. I am calling you first because this is a matter of extreme urgency."

"Oh, yeah?"

"You know," I say, fighting to hold it together, "I could say some terrible things to you right now. I could go low, speak out loud what I am holding inside, but I'm not going to do that. Instead, I'm going to tell you exactly what you're going to do. *Lose my daughter's number.* Then erase her from your mind. Don't ever contact her again. I mean *ever.* Do you understand me, young man?"

He sniffs. But when he speaks, I hear a hesitation. "How are you gonna make me do that?"

I exhale. "I'm being really nice to you right now. I'm being very, very controlled. I'm being considerate by giving you this phone call first as a courtesy. And now I'm giving you a warning. You are to lose her number."

He sniffs again. "Does Sydel know you're calling me?"

"Yes."

"What if I just hang up?"

"That's your choice. I am trying to give you the benefit of some knowledge. This is what's going to happen. Sydel is not going to have any further communication with you. If you try to contact her in any way, this will get really, really bad for you really, really fast. Call that a threat. I don't care. I call it a fact. Lose her number, young man. Do not contact her. Now I'm hanging up."

I click off, hold a moment, and dial his mother.

She answers her phone and tells me that she's putting me on speaker so her husband can hear our conversation. I wait for him to say hello, and then I get directly to it. I tell them how their son's behavior has crossed the line. I tell them that I called their son and told him never to contact Sydel again. I promise that as long as he never contacts her, this will end now. I tell them that out of courtesy and respect, I am calling them to explain their son's behavior. I want them to *know*. I don't yell and I don't threaten. But I am firm, steady, strong, and as serious as a heart attack.

"All right, thanks for letting us know," the young man's mother says.

"Bye," the father says, hanging up the phone.

"Goodbye," I say to silence.

Sydel never hears from that boy again.

In prayer, in reflection, in meditation, I find myself focusing on one persistent question.

Where do I want to be?

I want to be available to Sydel as much as she wants, as much as she needs. Of course, I don't admit out loud how much I need her. I see myself going to as many of her games as I can and staying closely connected to her when she comes home. We both need that connection.

And I need to be connected to Riley.

Riley Elizabeth Curry.

My granddaughter.

Stephen has met Ayesha, they have married, and I have gone from Mom to Grandma.

I have changed roles. I've moved on from trainer to coach. Recently, we've celebrated Riley's first birthday. Every day she grows exponentially. In a blink, she has grown from an infant to a little person, and I want to experience as much of her life as I can, as much as Stephen and Ayesha want and will allow. I remember pounding the thought into my kids' heads as they started spending more and more time with the opposite sex—*we don't date, we mate*. Once that happens, the result may be grandbabies.

So, Riley arrived in 2013, and then, close behind her, Ryan, her baby sister in 2015. Two grandbabies now, and when I pause to consider time, how fast and fleeting these days feel, I suddenly realize that Sydel has completed her junior year of college and, now, in 2016, has begun senior year. *Senior year?* Didn't we move her into her dorm room yesterday? Well, yes, except that yesterday turns out to have been three years ago.

The kids have scattered all over the country. Stephen, Ayesha, and the kids have settled in the Bay Area, Seth has signed with the Dallas Mavericks, and after graduating from college, Sydel, with the help of Ayesha, will be moving to Napa to learn to be a sommelier. Now, connecting with them, arranging to be with them, spending time with them, I feel both torn and guilty. When I'm at school, I long to be with my kids and grandbabies. When I take time off to be with my kids or grandbabies, I feel guilty that I'm not at school.

In my heart, I know what I have to do. I'm just giving myself time, waiting for the right moment, allowing the truth to settle in and for me to accept it, to embrace it. In Montessori terms, I have completed my task. The school that I started is flourishing. I stand in awe of what we've created from one small house and twenty acres of farmland. The school has now become its own well-oiled Big Machine. I adore the kids. I feel full being around them, watching them grow, seeing them blossom from prekindergarten children into caring, feeling, thoughtful young people. I see myself as an educator, serving these kids and their families. I know we are all made by God for a purpose. I have committed myself to empowering these kids and helping them discover their purpose. In a similar way, I love nurturing the teachers, seeing them develop as educators, watching them arrive with potential, and helping them find their purpose. However, now, I realize, in the deepest part of me, that my work has come to fruition. I have finished what I've started. I've come to the point that I need to move on.

In September, as school starts, I announce to the board and to the teachers and staff that I will be retiring in June, at the end of the school year. I want to end my more than two decades at the school my way, in true Sonya style, without fanfare and with no big celebration. I want to enjoy each day, each moment of the year. I want to take my time. I want to dawdle.

The year seems to sprint forward. Christmas comes, then New Year's, then Easter, and suddenly we've arrived at a few weeks before the school year ends. As the days pass, I feel myself slowing down, taking everything in. I walk through the buildings, savoring the kids' artwork on the walls, remembering when we had that one building in the middle of farmland. I take walks on the grounds. I don't take pictures. Somehow, I feel distanced from the moment when I take a picture. I want to be *in* every moment. I want to be as present as possible.

We come to our final year-end event, our annual spring picnic. This year, parents greet me carrying feelings of finality, of gravity. They say goodbye and thanks and wish me well. Some ask if I will be having a formal send-off, a farewell party, a banquet, a special commemorative evening.

"I won't," I say, gesturing at the kids running around. "This is it. All I really want. I just want to kind of say goodbye and move on. Part of life's process, I guess. I want to leave quietly. Kind of sneak away."

"What will you do now?" a parent asks.

"I don't know," I say. "I don't have a specific plan. Maybe I don't want one."

The last day of school arrives. I stay close to my office, taking everything in, trying to process this day, not wanting to give in to any emotion. As the day comes to an end, teachers and staff drop by, saying their tearful, solemn goodbyes. Meanwhile, all day a steady parade of kids marches through my office, insisting on hugs.

"We want to say goodbye to Miss Sonya," they say.

"We're not going to make a big deal out of this," I say. "Y'all get five seconds for a hug."

Grinning, I squeeze each one—most for longer than five seconds. *These kids*, I think, holding on to a hug, clinging to a moment.

Two decades.

So many kids.

My kids.

The day ends, and with it the end of an era. Nearly half my life, I think. Yet, heading to my car, I don't feel sad, or numb, or emotional.

I feel stoical and fulfilled. I know I've done the right thing at the right time. That has become clearer by the day, by the minute. I have completed this phase of my life. I will now have a reservoir of time to do what I want, when I want.

Over the summer, I pick a day when I know nobody will be around and I drive back to school to clean out my office. I enter the deserted building, take a deep breath, and walk through the empty hallway, my footsteps echoing off the halls. I go into my office and begin filling the cardboard boxes I've brought with me. I figure it will take a couple hours. It doesn't. It takes all day. I linger over each item before I place it into the box—photos, books, kids' artwork, notes kids wrote to me over the years, notes I wrote to myself, a coffee cup that I've had forever. I caress each item as if it's an heirloom, something precious, a memory that I want to cherish. I finally fill the cardboard boxes and carry them out to the car, one at a time. I start to walk back inside to see if I've forgotten anything, but I find myself standing frozen outside the front door to the school. I feel a weight dropping onto my chest. I heave a sigh, but I don't cry. I whisper to myself, to the heavens, "You're doing the right thing, Sonya, it's time."

I turn and head back to the car.

"Goodbye," I say to the school behind me.

My school.

Two months later, in September 2017, on what would be the first day of school, sitting in my living room, I break down.

I have kept my emotions locked up—until now. Suddenly, the dam bursts. Deep, body-rattling sobs rack me. I curl into a fetal position on the couch, my arms clutched around my middle, sobbing, gasping.

What did I do? I think. *Why did I leave?*
The realization follows.
School has started without me.
I'm not there.
I don't know where to be.
I need to find a new place.
I need a new purpose.

24

The Art of Living

2017.

Thanksgiving.

I have spent hours, days, weeks praying, trying to get in touch with where I am now, where I want to go, where I should be. I need to discover my purpose. My new purpose. I can't for the life of me find it.

I have defined myself as a mom. I have done all that I can. I have completed that task.

Life cannot be all about my kids, I think. *Can it?*

No.

I want to discover who else I can be. I don't want to be defined only by my kids or by my marriage.

But how can I be defined? What is my purpose?

You struggle to find your bearings. Finally, you pivot a certain way, face a new direction, feel it's right, commit, insist that you've found the way. But you have doubts. You shake them off. You're sure this is where you should go. You're positive. You go by your instinct and your experience, by how you've been taught your whole life, trained, by what you see—what you've always seen. You feel pulled toward that direction, toward that—thing, that place, that person—

Then, somehow, unbelievably, you find yourself somewhere *else*, in an entirely new place, a place you've never seen, a place you never knew existed. When you arrive there, you have an epiphany. You realize to your shock, "This is where I was supposed to be all along. This *is* the place."

As God says, "Sometimes I have to trick you."

This year for Thanksgiving, we have a new plan. Everyone will gather at Stephen's, including Seth and Sydel, who has settled in the Bay Area, and this year, Ayesha's family. Dell will be on the road, working basketball broadcasts for the Charlotte Hornets. Of course, I'll go. I love Thanksgiving. But I hesitate. I ask myself—

Where do I want to go?

What do I want to do?

Truthfully?

I want to be alone.

I want to chill.

I want to find somewhere where I can—

Pause. Breathe. Listen.

That's what this spa's website says.

Followed by—

The Art of Living Retreat.

Relax. Restore. Renew.

A place to meditate, be still, be quiet, in Boone, North Carolina, nestled in the Blue Ridge Mountains, promising peace, comfort, and quiet in the woods.

I have always felt drawn to the mountains. I find solace on higher ground, in the trees, in the cool, crisp mountain air. I close my eyes and I picture myself there—relaxing, sipping wine, journaling, taking some time for me, giving myself my own Thanksgiving.

"You're going *where?*"

Sydel can barely contain herself. I inch the phone away from my ear.

"I'm going to a spa," I say.

"Why?"

"I need—" I stop, swallow, try again. "I need some time. I want to chill, read, journal—"

"It's Thanksgiving. You love Thanksgiving."

"I do. Yes. I know. But Dad will be on the road. Everyone is scattered all over the country. I just feel that I want some time for myself. It's not a big deal. Four nights, five days in the mountains. I love the mountains."

"You'll be all alone."

"That's kind of the point."

"For Thanksgiving," Sydel says. "In the woods."

"I like the woods."

"Mom?"

"Yes?"

"This is weird."

Sydel's right. It is weird. What's even stranger is that I feel a step behind everything I do. I seem to be acting subconsciously. I know that I pack a bag, but I don't remember actually packing. I just see a suitcase packed on my bed. I know I map out the route to the retreat, but I don't remember plugging the directions into my phone. They simply appear in front of me, already punched in, Google mapped on my phone, ready for me to go. *You're here*, blinking green. Before I realize it, I'm in the car, driving, heading up to the mountains, an hour and forty-five minutes from my house. And each mile I go, each time I drive around a bend, the higher I feel myself climbing into the mountains, the happier I feel. I'm going straight up, nosing toward the sky, through the woods, driving toward the calmness of something that feels like heaven.

Sonya, I think, *this is exactly what you need.*

I stand in the lobby, trying to step to the front desk so I can check in, but I can't move. I feel my mouth open, freeze for a second, then snap shut. I take in the small lobby, slowly scan the room, the furnishings, the feel, and I think, *Rustic.*

Bordering on primitive.

I am far from the Four Seasons.

We're talking simple. Basic. No frills.

Rustic.

Clean, I'll say that.

I smile at the person behind the front desk and walk slowly toward her. Smiling broadly, but thinking, *Where am I?*

I check in.

I'm sure the rooms are better.

They're not.

A single bed. One flat pillow. No luxurious bedsheets. A thin, firm mattress. Wooden headboard. Wooden dresser. Wooden nightstand. Hard wood floors. No TV. No coffeemaker. Very basic bathroom.

Rustic.

Maybe this is their way of encouraging you to leave the room, go outside, explore nature.

I push my suitcase into the closet and realize that I'm famished. I glance at the brochure on the nightstand and read: "Dinner from five to seven." I have thirty minutes. If I hustle, I might make it.

I enter the dining room. Except it's not a dining room. It's a cafeteria. A few people stand at a buffet, easing their way down the food line, ladling what looks like a lot of vegetables onto their plates. People point. People nod. Nobody speaks.

Thursday night must be cafeteria night, I think.

I grab a plate and take my turn in the line. I smile at the woman in front of me, an older woman, gray hair, kind face. "Hello," I say.

The woman beams a smile back.

"So what do we have here tonight?" I ask pointing at the trays of food in front of us.

The woman shrugs and beams an even wider smile.

The woman must be hearing impaired, I think.

At some point during Montessori training, I may have learned a bit of sign language, but I don't remember anything now. Instead, I focus on the food, trying to figure out what I'm about to eat, and then I somehow realize, *Wait. This is all vegan food.* I see something that resembles chicken parmesan, but as I lean in to get a closer look, I don't see chicken or parmesan.

Yup, I say to myself, confirming. *Vegan.*

I'm so hungry I load my plate and then I find an empty table by the window. I glance around the cafeteria and I see a few people sitting together, a few others sitting by themselves. It takes me a minute to realize that nobody is speaking. The quiet at first feels heavy, like a thick fog over the room, but then I allow it to settle, and at least for dinner, I decide to go with it. I look at my plate of food—I'm a meat eater, maybe even a meat lover—so I hesitate. I'm fairly sure that in my life, I have never ordered vegan food on purpose. I start eating, tentatively, but as I chew, and eventually clean my plate, I think, with surprise, *This isn't bad. This vegan food's kind of cool. For tonight. For this one meal. No way I'll be eating this three times a day.*

I go back to my room, settle in for the night. I get as comfortable as I can in the very basic bed, pick up my pen and my journal, and open to a blank page. I begin to write but I abruptly stop, my hand hovering over the page. I sigh then, hugely. A sudden sadness wrenches me, grips me. I scan the room, think about where I am, and my lip starts to quiver. I look up at the ceiling, feeling my eyes fill up, and I say, "Oh, Lord, what have I done?"

Then I start to cry.

I'm alone—on Thanksgiving, without my family, without anyone—in this *rustic* retreat somewhere in the mountains, away from everybody, eating vegan food, drinking no alcohol, speaking no words, and then I lose it. I scream in silence—

What did I do? Where am I?

"Tomorrow," I say aloud, my spoken words jolting me between sobs, "I'm getting out of here."

I cry myself to sleep.

I wake up late, barely make it in time for breakfast. I again sit by myself, picking at my vegan breakfast—fake eggs, fake sausage, fake bacon—and then I dig in, and while I want to hate this food, I actually don't; I kind of like it, and I go back for seconds. Sitting in the quiet cafeteria, scrolling through my phone, I locate another spa's website, a place that's modern and luxurious, the type of experience I wanted to have, I planned to have, I thought I was going to have, serving real food, attended by people who I'm pretty sure are allowed to have a conversation, and I make a decision. I'll finish breakfast, pack my suitcase, and move to that place. But as I clean my plate, I begin leafing through today's schedule, and I notice that this place—The Art of Living—offers a combination yoga and meditation class right after breakfast, in a few minutes. I could make it. The class looks—inviting.

Well, I think, *as long as I'm here, I might as well give that class a shot. Then I'll go.*

I could seriously use some meditation, relaxing, chilling out. Besides, I've already paid for the day and a spa treatment later. I make a definite plan. Go to the class, do some yoga, meditate, or whatever—I'm actually not too sure how that works; I'm big on prayer, conversing with God, talking to God *aloud,* but I'm not fluent in meditation or relaxation, I'm too wired—I'll try this class, maybe the spa treatment, pack up my stuff, get in my car, and move on.

I love the class. I don't know if I meditate but I disappear. At first, I feel fidgety, a swirl of anxious, guilty, confused thoughts colliding, forming a traffic jam of emotions inside my head. I can't even find a focal point to calm myself or untangle the mess I'm obsessing over. Then something happens, and, *click,* I drift off into a kind of calmness. Serenity. It's like I began swimming in an icy cold river, fighting the frigid water at first, flailing, and then, suddenly, the water turns warm and soothing, and I stop fighting. My strokes go from flailing and desperate to smooth and easy. Suddenly, the water feels warm and relaxing. I don't think I fall asleep during the meditation, but maybe I do. The class ends, and I feel refreshed and energized. I bounce to my feet and start to head to the main lobby. I pull up in midstride, stopping to look at the view. The rolling hills and valleys tucked into the Blue Ridge Mountains are stunning, nearly knocking me breathless, and I think, *I am actually here, in this moment, experiencing this natural beauty. It's amazing that I live within two hours of this place.* A realization so obvious that I feel almost childish, and then I think, *No, not childish. Childlike. There's an enormous difference. You, Sonya, of all people know this. Childlike. Enjoy this sense of wonder. Most of all, keep it close. Never lose it.*

I reach into my bag, grab my journal, and scribble my thoughts, my thanks to God for giving me the gift of this class. Now I have to move on.

Before I check out, I stop at the front desk.

"Excuse me," I whisper to the young woman behind the desk, "I have a question."

"Yes?"

"Where am I?"

She smiles and shrugs and I realize that I have asked her a complicated question—maybe *the* deepest and most complicated question. I clarify.

"I mean, literally, where am I? What place is this?"

"It's a Shankara Ayurveda retreat. A wellness center."

"A silent wellness center, right?"

"Yes, exactly. Mind, body, spirit."

Then as if she senses I need further clarification she says, "Think about all the noise you encounter in your daily life. And not only noise coming from the outside world. The noises you hear within yourself, all these different voices telling you to do that or this, or to not do that or this. Voices of guilt, doubt, confusion, anger—"

"Those voices crash together and drown out your own voice," I say.

"Yes."

"You can't hear your own voice," I say, and then I think, *You can't hear His voice.*

Only in silence do you hear His voice.

That's why I'm here.

I need to hear His voice.

I focus now on the small voice that speaks to me across the front desk in the lobby. She has been saying something and, as if my ears have been blocked, I haven't been able to hear *her* voice.

"I'm sorry, I didn't hear—"

She laughs.

"I was saying, have you tried any Ayurveda body treatments?"

"No. I really just got here," I say, thinking, *And I will be checking out later.*

"Try the Abhyanga," she says.

"The—?"

"Abhyanga. Detoxifying warm oil massage. For your scalp."

"Really?"

"Oh, it's worth it," she says. "You won't believe it."

I will try it, I decide, after lunch, and *then* I'll pack up, check out, and drive over to the other place, the more traditional spa, and I will get pampered like crazy. I should make it there in time for a nice steak dinner, a big glass of wine, and some conversation.

But first I'll do the Abhyanga oil-on-my-head massage.

In a small room that reminds me of a sauna, I sit wrapped in a towel, my back to the young masseuse, her hands resting gently on my shoulders. She is explaining Abhyanga, using a soft, whispery voice. I focus only on certain words—*scalp, brain, nervous system, circulation, mindfulness,* and I feel myself nod because I have now gone silent—and then the young masseuse lifts a wooden bucket, and in a steady flow, pours a half gallon of oil over my head. I wince and narrow my eyes shut as the warm, soft oil sloshes over my hair, drips down my face, my hair sticking to my forehead, and then the masseuse slowly begins massaging my scalp and face. Her long fingers knead my scalp, working the oil in, the pungent smell of the oil wafting through the air. She works powerfully and gently at the same time, always in near slow motion, and as she kneads my scalp as if she's preparing bread dough, I feel as if I am being anointed.

What is happening to me? I think, a feeling of pleasure and then calm falling over me, and then I think—

This is holy.

I recall a verse from the Bible, James 5:14.

"Is anyone among you sick? Let them call the elders of the church to pray over them and anoint them with oil in the name of the Lord."

The oil itself has no healing power. That power comes from God.

With the oil dripping down my face, sticking to my scalp, the masseuse rubbing the oil in, I say to myself, *I am being cleansed. I am being anointed. I am being made holy.*

A smile sneaks across my face because I suddenly know—

I am supposed to be here. I can't leave. God brought me here.

God, I think, *You tricked me again.*

I decide to stay one more night—and then I'll go to the fancy spa and pamper myself.

But there's another meditation class and a nature walk and—

I never leave. I stay for the entire retreat. I eat vegan food three times a day. I retreat into silence. I embrace the quiet, realizing that I have to get quiet to hear His voice. I came seeking a purpose, asking myself the urgent questions, "Who am I? What is my purpose now?"

I discover during this retreat, in my silence, in my quiet, in my deep reflection, that you need to slow down, listen, close your mind, get out of the way, and allow God to guide you. Hear His voice. Listen.

Most of all, I learn this:

You will *not* find your purpose.

Your purpose will find you.

I leave the Art of Living in a state that goes above being high. I feel that something inside me—my soul—has shifted. I can't explain it but I feel it. I drive down the mountain road, my body shimmering, my nerve endings alive in a way that I have never felt before. My entire being crackles with electricity and serenity. I want to go back again and I want everyone I love to experience what I did. I know that Sydel will find the experience as life changing as I did.

As I drive, I feel ready for whatever purpose God has in store for me. I'm open in a way that I have also never felt. I know that I will be facing change, a life change, a seismic shift of my soul that will cause me and those around me to feel upended for a short time, but then I and all of us will land on sturdier, safer ground. I will take a leap of faith. I feel that, too. Of course, I would never leap without faith. My faith is what propels me, what causes the leap in the first place. I will always attempt to represent God. I know that whatever purpose presents itself will come from Him. I'm ready. I'm a little shaken—but I'm ready.

Suddenly, I arrive at a clearing in the woods and by instinct, without thinking at all, I pull over to a hiking trail. I can only see a bit of the trail because the path disappears into the woods. I sigh and then I shake my head. I have never gone hiking in my life. Never. Not one time. I have never had the remotest desire to hike—until this moment. I have to do this. I have to take this hike into the woods. Alone.

I step out of the car, lock the doors, grab a bottle of water, and laughing to the point that I almost crack myself up, I begin—*hiking.*

I hike for two hours.

As I walk, my mind clears. Thoughts swim in my head. Images come roaring in. I see my kids at every age, at every stage. I see pictures of myself as a child, living in the trailer park, teaching Philip to read, creating my own school with the little kids in the park, playing teacher, being a teacher. I see myself in high school and college, excelling at volleyball. I see the births of my children. I see places I have lived—Radford, Blacksburg, Salt Lake City, Cleveland, Charlotte. I see the creation of my school. I see moments of parenting, of being the mom I was destined to be, training my kids, taking them to church, bringing God home. I see myself prayer walking through the house. I see us all laughing, dancing, partying, praying, and laughing again, mostly laughing. I see all three of the kids graduating from high school and I see me taking all of them to college. I see Sydel leaving and I watch a reflection of myself breaking down. I see myself walking through the empty hallway of my school, my days as the head of school over, my task completed. I see all this and I realize—all this was the past. This was before. I am here now. I am new now.

The only thing we can control in our lives is our breathing.

If I've taken one thing away from the Art of Living, it would be that.

We can only react to what life throws at us, relying on, hoping for, praying for God's strength to help us through each challenge.

That is the key to parenting. That is how you dare to parent.

Prepare.

Pray.

Breathe.

Where am I?

I walk tentatively, feeling lost, adrift, and for a moment, fear grips me. I take a few more steps on the path, unsure of where I am going, and the fear abruptly dissolves, replaced by a sense of calm. I feel that God is walking with me, taking the journey by my side.

Late afternoon comes in and I begin to walk in shadows. I turn back, heading down the hiking trail toward the car. As I walk down the path, the only sound my own footsteps thumping on the ground, a thought jumps into my head and nestles into my mind. It lodges there and stays in place with a pleasant sort of buzz. I remain aware of the warmth of that feeling. Although the buzz makes me gasp a little, shakes me slightly, mostly, the thought—that buzz—makes me smile. I know exactly what that buzz is.

It's a realization. The reason for this hike. The message God has given me and I have received, although it may be a message I have not yet fully accepted. But I am about to.

Sonya, you have to write this book.

You have to share your family and your faith.

I get it, Lord. I hear You. Loud and clear. Did You have to stick me all the way up here, in these woods, on a *hike*? Did You think I wouldn't listen? I know. I know. You had to make sure You got my attention.

I got You.

Acknowledgments

FIRST, TO GOD: Thank you for loving, chastening, and caring for me all of my life. Thank you for being faithful to Your promise in Romans 8:28—"that God works all things together for the good of those who love Him, who are called according to His purpose." Without You, I would have been a coward to doubt and fear so many times.

To my children, Stephen, Seth, and Sydel:

I would like to thank God for blessing me with the responsibility of loving, nurturing, and raising you—and for letting me experience being a mom.

Thank you for trusting me, obeying, forgiving, and loving your dad and me as we stumbled through the ups and downs of being young parents. Thank you for your support and words of wisdom now that you are adults and have your own families as we navigate through our current challenges as your parents. Thank you for honoring your families and God with your children's lives.

I am honored to be your mom.

To Ayesha, Callie, and Damion: Thank you for loving my children and treating me like your real mom!

To Riley, Ryan, Canon, Carter, Cash, and Daxon: I love you all a bushel and a peck! You are "the crown of the aged..."—Proverbs 17:6.

Dell: Thank you for being a good provider and co-parent. You were always willing to go along with my sometimes "over-the-top" ideas whether you personally agreed or not.

To my mom, Candy Adams: Mom, I so admire your resilience and I cherish your huge heart. You are the backbone of our family and always there when I need a laugh!

To Daddy and my Adams family: Thank you for bringing me into your family and into your hearts.

To my siblings and my "Prayer Family": Ron and Jill, India and Tiffeny, and Lyrissa.

To Mimi and Will: You will always occupy a special place in my heart. I pray for you every day.

Thank you to the women in my life who set an example for me as moms and strong women.

To my late grandmother, Granny Evelyn; my mother-in-law, Juanita Curry, who set an exemplary example of how to be a mother-in-law; Aunt Lula, who showed me what it looked like to handle business inside and outside of the home—you are seen as a matriarch not only in our immediate family, but also in your community; Aunt Lois, for allowing me to tag along on all of your children's extracurricular activities; Nanny Marion, my godmom, for opening up your home and always being there whenever I needed anything; Judy Perrel, for adopting our family when we moved to Charlotte in 1988; Ms. Verna Stone, for spoiling my family rotten whenever we were with you; and Michelle Bain-Brink, my BFF—I couldn't do this thing called life without you.

Thank you to my teachers and coaches, in particular Ms. Pierce, my high school Spanish teacher. You motivated me to dream big and to not settle for less than what I deserved in life. You encouraged me to participate in a variety of activities in high school and make college a goal.

A special thanks to Coach John Pierce for giving me the opportunity to attend college. You were my biggest cheerleader in high school sports, helping me with college recruiting, and eventually becoming my volleyball coach at Virginia Tech.

To our nannies, Cindy Tolbert and Jackie Curry: Thank you.

It does take a village! Thank you to all of our friends and family members who helped with babysitting. Everyone knew that when you visited the Curry house, you had to work!

To my friends who supported me along the journey of writing this book, from offering encouragement, editing, reviewing, and advice—Tracy Chutorian Semler, Trini Perry, Ginger Eklund, and Toni Lovejoy.

Alan Eisenstock! Alan Eisenstock! Alan Eisenstock! Thank you for being such a good listener. You have a gift of capturing the true spirit of the author. I actually looked forward to our weekly meetings that usually turned into therapy sessions! You were appointed by God, and I am so thankful for you!

Finally, I want to thank the shepherds of this book.

Anthony Mattero, my extraordinary agent and number one champion of this book. Thank you for believing in me.

To everyone at HarperOne, with extra thanks to Maya Alpert for guiding the book through production.

My eternal gratitude goes to Shannon Welch and Gideon Weil. You shared my vision, you felt my heart, you heard my voice. Gideon, thanks for your patience, your gentle nudges, and having my back.

About the Author

SONYA CURRY is an entrepreneur, an educator, and the founder of the Christian Montessori School of Lake Norman in North Carolina. She is the mother of Stephen and Seth Curry and Sydel Curry-Lee. A member of the NBA Moms Organization, Sonya often speaks of her experiences as a mother, educator, and Christian, sharing her testimony about the love of Christ, parenting, and education.